Why is this *the* book that every mom a[...] hands? Because we do our best parentin[...] if you're like me, your parenting may sug[...] problem solving, worrying, and fixing. Jodie Berndt shares inspiring, tender, and humorous stories to demonstrate that the most powerful thing we can do for our children is pray, and she equips us to pray the power of God's Word over every aspect of their adult lives. The prayers woven into her books have blessed, protected, and enriched (in ways we likely don't even know!) the hearts and lives of our four boys.

JEANNIE CUNNION, author of *Mom Set Free*
and *Parenting the Wholehearted Child*

I love this book! You hold in your hands an amazing Scripture-saturated resource with real-life, true stories that will turn your fears into expectant hope. You have the opportunity of partnering with God in the destiny he has for your adult children through prayer.

FERN NICHOLS, founder of Moms in Prayer International

Once again, Jodie Berndt has done her homework. As the mother of seven grown children, five of whom have added their spouses to our family mix, I read each chapter of this book with a heart hungry for encouragement and hope. I wasn't disappointed! I have been reinvigorated to "take my stand at the wall" and believe God for *my* children, their spouses, and my grandchildren. Thank you, Jodie, I needed this!

TERRY MEEUWSEN, cohost of *The 700 Club*
and founder of Orphan's Promise

Jodie Berndt's books, *Praying the Scriptures for Your Children* and *Praying the Scriptures for Your Teen*, were on our bedside table for almost two decades. We prayed through a different chapter every night. All the peaceful sleep we had raising five kids we owe to God, who met us through the prayers Jodie so wisely crafted. We are overjoyed to continue this journey of trusting God as we read *Praying the Scriptures for Your Adult Children*.

MARK AND SUSAN MERRILL, founders of Family First and authors of *The Passionate Mom* and *All Pro Dad*

Jodie Berndt has written a magnum opus for everyone who wants a practical way to pray for their adult kids. Her book is filled with stories and real-life situations that clearly identify issues every child will encounter and then lays out a praying plan to address those issues with wisdom, biblical counsel, and practical parental advice. This book will become your constant companion for many years as your children go through all the stages of their lives. Well done, Jodie!

JOE BATTAGLIA, broadcaster, author of *The Politically Incorrect Jesus*, and president of Renaissance Communications

Jodie Berndt knows what it's like to have to trust God in the tricky places—those seasons when outcomes are uncertain or when our children's lives don't look like we thought they would. She takes us by the hand and—with wisdom, compassion, and a dose of her trademark good humor—leads us straight to God's throne and gives us a biblically based template to express our heart's deepest longings. *Praying the Scriptures for Your Adult Children* invites you to slip your hand into God's and pray with confidence, trusting him to hear your cry, accomplish his purposes, and give you his peace.

SUSAN A YATES, author of *Risky Faith* and
Raising Kids with Character That Lasts

Jodie Berndt provides invaluable wisdom and encouragement to keep you spiritually connected with your adult children. She invites you to slip your hand into God's to join him in the work he keeps on doing after they leave the safety and comfort of your home. Chapter by chapter, she equips you with the necessary tools to pray Word-filled, character-shaping, life-transforming prayers for the children who have left the nest but not your heart.

WENDY BLIGHT, Proverbs 31 First 5 writing team, Bible teacher, and author of *I Know His Name* and *Living So That*

Parents, read this book! It might not make you a faster runner, but it will give you a leg up in praying God's Word powerfully for your adult children. You will gain a peace and a sense of purpose as you parent your children on your knees in prayer.

HONORABLE JIM RYUN, Olympic medalist and world record holder in the mile, former congressman, and author of *In Quest of Gold*

This is the best kind of book—one you pray-read because it informs your mind while also invoking your prayers. I found myself devouring Jodie Berndt's unassuming (but wise) insight and then pausing to pray the Scripture she lists. And then I would read again. And then stop to pray. This book will never make it to my bookshelf, because it has already found a permanent home on my bedside table. I'll pray-read it again and again. (And—psst—these pages are for parents with children of all ages, like mine are, not just those with grown children.)

SARA HAGERTY, author of *Every Bitter Thing Is Sweet* and *Unseen*

PRAYING
the SCRIPTURES
for Your
Adult Children

Trusting God with the Ones You Love

JODIE BERNDT

ZONDERVAN

Praying the Scriptures for Your Adult Children
Copyright © 2017 by Jodie Berndt

Requests for information should be addressed to:
Zondervan, *3900 Sparks Dr. SE, Grand Rapids, Michigan 49546*

ISBN 978-0-310-34807-8 (ebook)

Library of Congress Cataloging-in-Publication Data

Names: Berndt, Jodie, author.
Title: Praying the Scriptures for your adult children : trusting God with the ones you love / Jodie Berndt.
Description: Grand Rapids, Michigan : Zondervan, [2017] | Includes bibliographical references.
Identifiers: LCCN 2017020130 | ISBN 9780310348047 (softcover)
Subjects: LCSH: Mothers--Prayers and devotions. | Adult children--Religious life. | Bible--
  Devotional literature.
Classification: LCC BV4847 .B447 2017 | DDC 248.3/2085--dc23 LC record available at https://
  lccn.loc.gov/2017020130

Cover design: Curt Diepenhorst
Cover photo: Sarah Robertson / imagebearerphotography.com / Getty Images ®
Interior design: Kait Lamphere

First printing October 2017 / Printed in the United States of America

23 24 25 26 27 LBC 30 29 28 27 26

To my husband, Robbie—
with love and gratitude for your prayers
and for all the ways
you continually point our family
toward God's faithfulness.

And to the moms and dads who so graciously
shared their stories for this book—

Thank you.

May God make you worthy of his calling, and by his
power may he bring to fruition your every desire for
goodness and your every deed prompted by faith.

2 Thessalonians 1:11

Contents

Foreword

Parenting is one of the toughest jobs in the world, and today's culture isn't making it any easier. At Focus on the Family, we hear from parents every day who are asking for help with any number of issues involving their kids. And when we feel like we're struggling, it can be tempting to throw up our hands and simply declare, "All I can do now is pray!"

But how often do we forget that prayer is our *first* line of defense? We should be lifting our kids before the Lord constantly, in both good times and bad, knowing that our prayers yield fruit in ways we can't begin to imagine. Storming the gates of heaven for our kids is never an exercise in futility, and, thankfully, there's a wealth of guidance within the pages of Scripture.

My friend Jodie Berndt is passionate about this message. Time and again, she has seen what the Lord can do in response to fervent and faithful prayer, and now she is offering invaluable encouragement to parents of adult children.

Once our kids have "flown the nest," our parenting will change dramatically, but our sons and daughters will always need our prayers. Whether they are facing unemployment, struggling through marital discord, grieving over infertility, caught up in an addiction, or confronting other life challenges, it's vital that we continue interceding on their behalf. Our role in our kids' lives may be different once they're living on their own, but there is great assurance in the knowledge that our children have a Father in heaven who walks beside them through all of life's ups and downs.

My wife, Jean, and I are staring an empty nest in the face. Our boys are both in high school, and it won't be long before they're heading off to chart their own courses. We have poured our blood, sweat, and tears into parenting our sons—and, yes, countless hours of prayer as well. I'd be lying if I said I wasn't a bit nervous about seeing Trent and Troy on the brink of adulthood.

As Jodie reminds us, however, our work isn't done when our kids leave home—and we do some of our best parenting on our knees.

Jodie wants to see you embrace God's vision for your adult children. She longs for you to rest in the certainty that you have not launched your child into the world alone and unprotected. To the contrary, our kids have a tender and sovereign Provider and Protector, a God who will never leave them or forsake them (Deuteronomy 31:8).

Prayer is one of the most important parenting assignments we've been given. It is an eternal investment in our kids' hearts and souls, and we must never underestimate its impact. As you delve into Jodie's book, get ready to gain a renewed commitment to this all-important calling!

JIM DALY, president of
Focus on the Family

PART 1

PRAYING

for Your

ADULT CHILD

CHAPTER 1

The Battle Begins

Remember the Lord, who is great and awesome,
and fight for your families, your sons and
your daughters, your wives and your homes.

Nehemiah 4:14

My husband, Robbie, and I take a long weekend every year to get away with four other couples. We all live in different parts of the country and it's not uncommon for us to go for months without seeing or even talking to one another, but we're united by at least three common bonds: we're all empty nesters; we've known each other since our kids were very young; and we believe in the power of prayer.

And there's one other thing. If someone were to write a how-to book on Christian parenting (the kind that listed all the things you are supposed to do to get your kids to turn out "right"), all of us would probably be in it. Take your kids to church? Check. Send them to Christian camps in the summertime? Done. Give your time and your money to ministries like Focus on the

Family, Young Life, Fellowship of Christian Athletes, or Passion Conferences? We were all over stuff like that.

And more. We had family devotions at breakfast. Bedtime prayers at night. Scripture memory cards on the fridge, right next to the chore chart. Hey, Robbie and I even dressed our son up as Bibleman for Halloween. It was a real costume that came with a cape and a big plastic sword, and we wrote verses on little slips of paper so he could give them to people when he took their Kit Kats.

You don't get much more Christian than that.

You would think, given all of this Really Good Parenting, that the five of us couples would have some golden children. And, thanks to God's grace, we do, particularly when we remember verses like Philippians 1:6, which remind us to leave room for God to finish writing their stories. But as the ten of us sat around the dinner table during one of our autumn getaways, sharing the joys and heartaches of our lives, it became clear that nobody was out of the woods. All of us were praying about something (or a bunch of things) in our kids' lives. All of us were counting on God's mercy and his love.

One adult child was living with his girlfriend. Another struggled with a crippling addiction. Several of our kids needed jobs. A couple of them were doing the boomerang thing, bringing their lives and their laundry back home. We were concerned about things like infertility, alcohol abuse, iffy dating relationships, emotional and mental health, money troubles, spiritual uncertainty, and more than one case of what our grandparents might have simply called "wild living."

Goodness, I longed for the days when I got called into the principal's office because little Robbie had tied his shoelaces together in the library and made the other kids laugh, or because Virginia had been caught throwing tennis balls at the football team during practice.

The good news is that the same God who watched over my kids' lives back then—back when their issues didn't seem quite so complex or life-shaping—is still looking out for them today. I may get tired, discouraged, or confused in the spiritual whack-a-mole exercise that is parenting adult children, but God doesn't. "He will not grow tired or weary, and his understanding no one can fathom."[1]

Prayer Principle

The things you give to God in prayer—your worries, concerns, and needs—are the ties that bind your heart to his. Our struggles are his entry points.

And the *really* good news is that these very struggles—the money troubles, the rocky relationships, the substance abuse, the spiritual doubt, and all of the other things that keep us up

---

1. Isaiah 40:28.

at night and make us wonder what lies in store for our child's future—are the ties that forever bind our heart to God's. Our struggles are his entry points. And, as my friend Lisa's mom likes to remind her kids as they parent *their* kids, "Children improve your prayer life."

I still love what Jack Hayford said about prayer (I quoted him in the first few pages of *Praying the Scriptures for Your Children*). Prayer, he said, is a "partnership of the redeemed child of God working hand in hand with God toward the realization of his redemptive purposes on earth."[2] What a privilege it is for us, as parents, to be able to slip our hand into the hand of our heavenly Father and join him in the continuing work that he is doing in our adult children's lives. And what a joy, as we allow the words of Scripture to shape our perspective and transform our prayers, to be given a window into God's heart.

If you've read *Praying the Scriptures for Your Children* or *Praying the Scriptures for Your Teens*, you know why I like to use the Bible as the basis for my prayers. I love the intentional, purpose-driven nature of verses like Isaiah 55:11, which promise that God's Word will not return empty, but will accomplish what he desires and achieve his purposes. I love the strength and power of Hebrews 4:12, which likens Scripture to a sword, one that is "alive and active" as it goes to work on our thoughts and our attitudes. And I think that advice about prayer doesn't

---

2. Jack Hayford, *Prayer Is Invading the Impossible* (South Plainfield, NJ: Logos, 1977), 92.

get much more straightforward than John 15:7, where Jesus says that if we remain in him and his words remain in us, we can ask for whatever we wish and it will be done for us. This isn't some sort of "name it, claim it" trick; rather, it just makes sense that the more we press into Christ and allow the Bible to shape our thoughts and desires, the more our requests will line up with what God wants to do—with the goal being that we bring glory to God and live our lives according to his design (John 15:8).

===================== *Prayer Principle* =====================

The more we allow the Bible to shape our prayers, the more our requests will line up with God's plans.

But here's the thing about praying for our adult children. It's hard. It's not just the whack-a-mole nature of parenting that makes it tough. As seasoned moms and dads, we are used to fighting simultaneous battles on many fronts. Praying for our adult children is hard for at least two other reasons.

First (and obviously), the *issues* are harder. When my friend Sally learned that her first-grade son had been swiping crayons from the Sunday school closet, she was concerned; when he grew up and got mixed up with a gang in a faraway city, she was devastated. The problems and challenges that color our adult children's lives and relationships are serious and often have long-term consequences. No longer can we as parents sit on the prayer bench and watch the JV squad play. Like it or not, we've got a starting spot on the varsity team.

But that's not all. The other (less obvious) thing that makes praying for our adult children tough is that, as empty nesters whose kids are often scattered all over the country (or even the world), most of us don't have a parenting community. We can't sit in the park and ask another mom for advice while our children play on the monkey bars. We no longer find ourselves forging bonds with other parents at the middle school fund-raiser or on the sidelines of the high school football game. Without even realizing there was a shift, we may find ourselves missing those easy, organic relationships built around the simple fact that we are in a common season, relationships that can open the door to mutual encouragement, laughter, and hope. We are, perhaps for the first time in twenty or thirty years, kind of alone.

Which is where this book comes in.

All of the characters in this book are real people. I've changed names and minor details to protect their privacy (except where I talk about my own family members, who are generally good sports with thick skin), but their stories are all true. I don't share them so that you can compare yourself (I have a friend who watches *Hoarders* just to make herself feel better about her own storage problems); rather, I've interviewed people and recorded God's faithfulness in their lives because I want you to know at least three things:

First, *you are not alone.* There is no "perfect" family. Everyone—

even that beautiful woman who sits across the aisle from you at church, the one with the daughter who just got engaged and the son who just got promoted—has issues. And nobody has done it "right." When it comes to raising our children and pursuing God's best for their lives, we all need huge buckets of his grace, and we are all in this together.

=== *Prayer Principle* ===

It's never too late to start praying
God's best for your children.

Second, *it's not too late.* When *Praying the Scriptures for Your Children* came out, I can't tell you how many people told me they'd wished they'd had the book when their kids were younger. Well, guess what? Most of the people who shared their stories for this book didn't have that resource either, and for a lot of them, using the Bible to animate their prayer life is a fairly new and unfamiliar strategy. But they're doing it—and so can you. It's never too late. And as you'll see in some of the stories ahead, God is all about making up for lost time and dishing up some retroactive blessings.[3]

And finally, *you really can have peace*, even in life's messiest moments. Jesus told us we'd have trouble, but he tucked those words inside two of the most beautiful promises in the Bible.

---

3. Joel 2:25.

Here's how John 16:33 reads (and I've added italics, so you can see the tuck): "I have told you these things, so that *in me you may have peace.* In this world you will have trouble. *But take heart! I have overcome the world.*"

As we pray and parent together, let's stretch across the trouble in our lives, using one hand to grab hold of God's peace and the other to grasp on to his victory—even if we don't see the answer just yet.

In the pages ahead, I will share joyful stories of answered prayer—lives changed, relationships healed, troubles resolved. But I will also recount the struggles of parents who are still in the thick of it, moms and dads who are choosing to put their trust in God, even when the outcome is uncertain. My prayer is that both types of stories will serve to build your faith, give you hope, and (as you trust God with your own adult children) improve your prayer life.

You are welcome to skip right to the chapter that best reflects your particular need, but I also encourage you to read this book in its entirety, since every issue brings up spiritual truths and principles you can apply to a variety of situations. And yes, the circumstances our children face may be harder than when they were young, but we can hold on to this truth: God has not changed. He is still (and always will be) the Father who loves us enough, and is powerful enough, to do immeasurably more than all we could ask or imagine.[4]

---

4. Ephesians 3:20.

Poised for Prayer

Being a Virginia Beach girl, I love the picture on the cover of this book. I like the *sand*, which makes me think of children, since it reminds me of God's promise to Abraham about his descendants; the *ocean*, because in the Bible, water is often a symbol for God's Word; and the *hint of sunshine* in the sky, which seems to beckon us into the light of God's love.

Most of all, though, I like the gate.

Back when Nehemiah was rebuilding the walls and gates of Jerusalem, he stationed people to guard the exposed places, "posting them by families, with their swords, spears and bows."[5] And when the enemy showed up and threatened to attack, Nehemiah told the Israelites not to be afraid. Instead, he said, "Remember the Lord, who is great and awesome, and fight for your families, your sons and your daughters, your wives and your homes."[6]

We must do the same thing today. We must fight for our families, guarding the gates of our homes. We may not have swords and spears, but our weapons are even more powerful. We fight with God's Word and with prayer.

Like the chapters in *Praying the Scriptures for Your Children* and *Praying the Scriptures for Your Teens*, each chapter in this book ends with about a dozen Bible verses you can turn into personalized prayers for your children. But in talking with the

---

5. Nehemiah 4:13.
6. Nehemiah 4:14.

moms and dads who shared their stories with me, I realized that our kids aren't the only ones who need prayer. We do too. And even the most faith-filled believer will find himself or herself growing weary or even discouraged at times. It doesn't matter how old your children are. You never stop being a parent. You never stop caring.

And so, in addition to the Scripture prayers listed for our children, I've included a few verses at the end of each chapter that we can use to pray for ourselves. Let these words point you toward God's faithfulness, knowing that no word from God will ever fail.[7]

Prayer is a battle, and every warrior gets tired. Remember, though: You are not alone. And if you have an answered prayer or a verse that might help others (or even a prayer request that you don't mind putting out there for others to carry), I hope you'll join me at www.jodieberndt.com, where you'll find weekly prayer prompts and an opportunity to encourage others by posting your own comments. Together, we can do what Aaron and Hur did for Moses when the lives of God's children were at stake.[8] We can come alongside one another in prayer, lifting up each other's hands as we tap into the words first breathed by the Father—words that speak his love and his promises into our lives.

---

7. Luke 1:37.

8. When the Amalekites attacked the Israelites, Moses watched the battle from the top of a hill. As long as he held up his hands, the Israelites were winning. But when Moses grew tired, the battle turned. That's when Aaron and Hur stepped in to hold up Moses's arms, Aaron on one side and Hur on the other. "His hands remained steady till sunset," and the Israelites won (Exodus 17:8–13).

Prayers You Can Use

Most of the prayers in this book are for your children.
But as we close this chapter—as we prepare to guard the
gates—I want to share some of the promises I have prayed
for myself over the years. And I have prayed these verses
for you as I've worked on this book. I have asked God
to equip you for the battle, to give you strength when
the night feels dark and long, and to let you know how
immeasurably much you are loved.

Heavenly Father . . .

*You are the God of hope. Fill my heart with joy and peace
as I trust in you, so that I may overflow with hope by the
power of the Holy Spirit.*   ROMANS 15:13

*Remind me, when I am weary and burdened, that I can
come to you and find rest.*   MATTHEW 11:28

*Make me worthy of your calling, and by your power bring
to fruition every desire I have for goodness and every deed
that is prompted by faith.*   2 THESSALONIANS 1:11

Thank you for interceding for my children and for me. Help me remember that nothing can separate us from your love. ROMANS 8:34–39

Equip me to be joyful in hope, patient in affliction, and faithful in prayer. ROMANS 12:12

Teach me to approach your throne of grace with confidence so that I may receive mercy and find grace to help me in my time of need. HEBREWS 4:16

Help me not to worry about anything, but to pray about everything and to thank you for all you have done. May your peace, which exceeds understanding, guard my heart and my mind. PHILIPPIANS 4:6–7 NLT

When I feel discouraged or when the answer seems to be a long time in coming, strengthen me so that I will always pray and not give up. LUKE 18:1

Enable me to stand firm so that nothing will move me. Help me give myself fully to the work of prayer, knowing that this labor is not in vain. 1 CORINTHIANS 15:58

When I come before you, Lord, let it be with thanksgiving and praise because you are good, your love endures forever, and your faithfulness continues to all generations.

PSALM 100:4–5

Show me how to wrestle in prayer for my children, that they may stand firm in all the will of God, mature and fully assured.   COLOSSIANS 4:12

Lord, teach me to pray.   LUKE 11:1

CHAPTER 2

Blessing and Releasing Your Adult Child

"The LORD bless you
and keep you;
the LORD make his face shine on you
and be gracious to you;
the LORD turn his face toward you
and give you peace."

NUMBERS 6:24–26

One of the best things about being a parent is getting to watch your child grow up.

That's also one of the hardest things, particularly when the paths our kids choose don't line up with our vision for what their "happiness" is supposed to look like or when we aren't really sure what God's best plan is for their lives. We want our children to become the people God meant for them to be ("God's handiwork, created in Christ Jesus to do good works, which

God prepared in advance"[1]), but the shape of this God-sketched design can take a lot of different forms. And as our grown-up children make decisions that will impact their future, our prayers for their well-being will be as varied and diverse as they are.

There is one prayer, though, that every one of our kids can use. It's the prayer of blessing, and as we release our adult children into the grown-up world of colleges and careers and families of their own, this prayer represents a surefire way we can influence their lives and partner with God as he works to accomplish his good purposes.

Prayer Principle

Our adult children have different needs, but all of them can use the prayer of blessing.

In their book *The Love Dare for Parents*, brothers Stephen and Alex Kendrick say that to bless someone means to "speak well" of that person. In family life, they write, it's "a parent using their God-given authority to verbally affirm their children for who they are, while also encouraging and inspiring them toward future success."[2] There is no age limit on this kind of affirmation, and as I interviewed moms and dads for this chapter, I got a

---

1. Ephesians 2:10.
2. Stephen and Alex Kendrick, *The Love Dare for Parents* (Nashville: B&H, 2013), 161.

front-row seat into the way the prayer of blessing can lay the groundwork for God to move, even when our own hearts are heavy or we don't see evidence of God's provision.

One mom told me how sad she was that her thirty-four-year-old daughter was still single. "I want her to enjoy the gift of marriage," she said, "and I know she wants that too. So I am asking God to provide a husband for her, but I am also thanking him for the good things he has already poured into her life: her leadership skills, her honesty, her compassion, and even the fact that she is as comfortable working in a soup kitchen as she is attending a fund-raising gala in an evening gown!"

Recognizing the weight that words can carry ("The tongue has the power of life and death," reads Proverbs 18:21), this wise mother looks for opportunities to highlight the ways she sees God using her daughter's gifts and talents. As a result of this affirmation, the young woman doesn't see herself as overlooked or somehow inferior to her married peers. Instead, she exudes joy and confidence, along with a healthy self-esteem that comes from knowing she is loved, and that her life has value and purpose.

Another mom shared her devastation when her college-aged son told her he was gay. "I searched the Bible to find anything that might convince me that homosexuality was not the sin I'd been taught it was," she said, "but I couldn't find any passages to support that view. I knew God loved my son as much as I did, but I didn't know what I was supposed to say or do."

Love him. That's what this dear mama felt God whisper to

her spirit. *You can't control your son's choices or his lifestyle; leave that to me. You just love him.*

Emboldened by that God-given freedom to exchange her worry for trust, she took a straightforward approach to blessing her son. "I told him the same thing I would tell a heterosexual child: he should honor God with his body, not engaging in any sexual relationships outside of marriage. But I didn't make my love conditional on whether he followed that advice. Instead, I let him know how grateful I was for things like his sense of humor and his intellect and for how I saw God using those gifts in his life.

"I imagine that plenty of kids his age are experimenting with who they are, what they believe, or where they get their sense of identity," she went on. "I'm praying that my son will find his identity in Christ, and that God will shape him into the man he wants him to be."

Here again, a mother's words—and her prayers—created a climate in which love and faith could flourish and relationships could grow.

If it seems awkward to bless an adult child who is not walking with the Lord or who has made a choice that we believe runs counter to God's commands, consider this: a blessing is not the same thing as an endorsement. Rather, when we bless our children, we do the same thing that God does when he blesses us: He forecasts his favor and guides us toward the abundant life he wants us to enjoy. The prayer of blessing is an acknowledgment that we are not trying to control our children's future; rather, we are handing that over to God and trusting him to give them a vision for using their talents and abilities, as well as a sense of purpose in life.

======================= *Prayer Principle* =======================

A blessing is not the same thing as an endorsement.
It's a way of handing our children's future over to God.

It's never too early to start blessing your children; consider Hannah's words when she brought her young son Samuel to the temple: "For his whole life he will be given over to the LORD."[3] Likewise—and perhaps more importantly—*it's never too late*. Scripture is brimming with accounts of blessings given to adults: Isaac blessing Esau and Jacob, Moses teaching the high priests how to bless the people of Israel, and even God blessing Jesus on the day he was baptized: "You are my Son, whom I love; with you I am well pleased."[4]

For Christ, this blessing marked the start of his adult ministry, the time when he would begin to attract the attention of both followers and foes. For our own children too, the prayer of *blessing* often involves a corresponding prayer of *release* into a world where they might face opposition, uncertainty, or any number of new and unfamiliar challenges.

One West Coast mom, Lisa, told me how hard it was when

---

3. 1 Samuel 1:28.
4. Genesis 27; Numbers 6:22–27; Mark 1:11.

her daughter took a new job in Boston. What if she got lonely? Or sick? What if she wandered away from her faith? The three-thousand-mile separation meant they would not see each other often; would their family remain close?

Lisa is a self-described "natural worrier." She could have easily given in to fear. Instead, she chose to release her daughter into God's protective arms and affirm what she saw him doing. He had opened the door to a job that combined her daughter's educational training with her artistic passion. Lisa knew she'd miss her girl, but even as she asked God to comfort her own heart, she prayed that he would cover her daughter with favor, establishing the creative work of her hands and making her efforts successful.[5] And if her daughter were to fall in some way—whether spiritually or in her career, her friendships, or something else—Lisa relied on the promise that God made to his people in Deuteronomy 33:27, where he said he would be their dwelling place and that his everlasting arms would be underneath them. Lisa loved that image. She prayed that if her daughter fell, God's strong arms would be right there to catch her.

———————

Sometimes this "blessing and releasing" process means letting go of our own hopes and dreams for our child's future.

Warren is the president and founder of an international

———————

5. Psalm 90:17.

ministry that brings health care, education, job training, and the gospel message to some of the most spiritually and physically inaccessible parts of the world. He has two sons, both of whom grew up participating in short-term mission trips. As the boys reached adulthood, Warren hoped that one (or both) of them might want to join him, professionally, in ministry. But he knew better than to push for that outcome.

"I've seen too many of my friends—people in business and in ministry—put the burden of succession on their children, regardless of the son's or daughter's intellectual ability, educational training, or even interest in what their parents are doing," he said. "Of course I've been tempted to pray that my sons would join me in my work, but I know that's just my own selfish itch. So instead, I have prayed that they would join God in his business— whatever that is—even if it means I have to push them or release them away from me to find their own journey."

=========== *Prayer Principle* ===========

As you pray God's blessing on your children,
release your plans and trust God to accomplish his.

Part of that pushing, Warren says, is helping his sons identify their strengths. "One of my boys has a strong entrepreneurial streak, and the other is really gifted at numbers and analysis," he says. "I've told them I'm praying 1 Peter 4:10 over their lives and careers, that God will equip them to use the gifts they have received to serve others and administer his grace. My sons might not wind up in full-time ministry, but that doesn't mean God can't use them to promote his kingdom."

Poised for Prayer

One of the Bible's best-known blessings is when God tells Abraham to leave his own country and go to a new land. "I will make you into a great nation," God promises, "and I will bless you; I will make your name great . . . All peoples on earth will be blessed through you."[6]

The ultimate fulfillment of this blessing, of course, is found in Jesus, Abraham's descendant and the Word who "became flesh and made his dwelling among us."[7] One of the things this Word-made-flesh promise says to me is that when we speak God's Word over our children—taking the Scriptures and using them as prayers of blessing—we are literally covering them with the presence of Christ.

When our children were little, Robbie and I would tuck them into bed with a lullaby. Some were songs we had learned at church; others were just Bible verses we put to tunes we made up (using enthusiasm, or even volume, to bridge the gaps in our musical talent). Their runaway favorite was an excerpt from

---

6. Genesis 12:1–3.
7. John 1:14.

Psalm 139. The song didn't have a formal title; the kids just called it "Presence."

Here are the lyrics:

> *Where can I go from your Spirit?*
> *Where can I flee from your presence?*
> *If I go up to heaven, you're there;*
> *if I make my bed in the depths, you are there.*
> *If I rise on the wings of the dawn,*
> *if I settle on the far side of the sea,*
> *even there your hand will guide me,*
> *your right hand will hold me fast.*

Robbie and I didn't know it then (and honestly, we were just trying to get the kids to fall asleep), but we were imprinting God's richest blessing on their hearts and minds: *the gift of his presence.*

In the chapters to come, you'll meet parents who've prayed their adult children through some of life's hardest seasons, from broken relationships and financial setbacks to mental health challenges and addictions. The ability to sense God's nearness, to be able to come into his presence and approach his throne of grace with confidence—in the good times, as well as in life's long, strength-sapping battles—is what gave these parents hope. It's what strengthened them. It's what gave them joy, even when they could see no earthly reason to rejoice.

And that's my prayer for all of us as we continue to love and pray for our children: *that we would know the presence, and the grace, of God*. It doesn't matter whether you feel like you have done everything "right" (and now find yourself wondering why things didn't turn out the way you thought they would) or whether you are all too aware of your failings (and now find yourself wondering if things will *ever* get better); all of us need God's grace in our lives. All of us need his presence.

Pray God's blessing—his presence—over your children. And as you do, "May the Lord of peace himself give you peace at all times and in every way. May the Lord be with you."[8]

---

8. 2 Thessalonians 3:16.

Prayers You Can Use

For Yourself

Heavenly Father . . .

Let my words be helpful for building my children up according to their needs, so that what I say will be a benefit to them.   EPHESIANS 4:29

Give me a wise heart, so that my words will be gracious like a honeycomb, bringing sweetness and health to my family.   PROVERBS 16:23–24

Let your presence go with me, and give me rest.   EXODUS 33:14

For Your Children

Heavenly Father . . .

Bless _____ and keep him; may your face shine on him. Turn your face toward _____ and give him peace.   NUMBERS 6:24–26

*Fulfill your purpose in _____. Give her a rich and
satisfying life.*   JOHN 10:10 NLT

*May your Spirit be with _____ wherever he goes. Guide
him and hold him fast.*   PSALM 139:7–10

*Be with _____. Save her and take great delight in her.
Quiet _____ by your love, and rejoice over her with
singing.*   ZEPHANIAH 3:17 NIV, ESV

*Pour out your Spirit on _____ and your blessing on his
descendants.*   ISAIAH 44:3

*Fill _____ with all joy and peace as she trusts in you
so that she may overflow with hope by the power of the
Holy Spirit.*   ROMANS 15:13

*Let grace and peace be _____'s in abundance. Give him
everything he needs for a godly life, and may he know that
he has been called by you.*   2 PETER 1:2–3

*May _____ and her descendants be known among the
nations, and may all who see them acknowledge that they
are a people the Lord has blessed.*   ISAIAH 61:9*

Give _____ a singleness of heart and action, so that she will always fear you and that all will then go well for her and for her children.   Jeremiah 32:39

May _____ be blessed as one who does not walk in step with the wicked, but delights in your law. May he be like a tree planted by streams of water, yielding fruit and prospering in whatever he does.   Psalm 1:1–3

Wherever _____ goes, be her secure dwelling place. Place your everlasting arms around and underneath her.

Deuteronomy 33:27 ESV

May loyalty and kindness be written on _____'s heart so that he will find favor and high regard in the sight of God and man.   Proverbs 3:3–4 CSB

CHAPTER 3

Praying for Your Child's Transition to Adulthood

When I was a child, I spoke and thought
and reasoned as a child. But when I
grew up, I put away childish things.
1 CORINTHIANS 13:11 NLT

When I grew up, I put away childish things. That's how the New Living Translation renders 1 Corinthians 13:11. Paul is talking about spiritual maturity, but his comparison to how children talk and think works. "Children live for the temporary," notes Warren Wiersbe in his commentary on this passage. "Adults live for the permanent."[1]

Never, perhaps, has the transition from the temporary to the permanent been so long in coming or marked by so many different paths as it is today. The traditional markers of adulthood—finishing school, leaving home, landing a job,

---

1. Warren W. Wiersbe, *The Wiersbe Bible Commentary: The Complete New Testament in One Volume* (Colorado Springs: Cook, 2007), 488.

getting married, and having children—are no longer as tidy and predictable as they used to be, and it's not at all uncommon to find young people taking these steps out of order, opting to skip some entirely, or even moving backward (by conventional linear standards) as they figure out who they want to be with and what they really want to do with their lives.

Which can be hard, sometimes, for parents. I remember my husband's comment when one of our children's friends turned down what looked like a very good job offer because it didn't sound all that fun. "It's probably not," Robbie agreed. "That's why they call it *work*." Much more gracious was the response from my friend's very Southern, very proper grandmother when she heard that one of her grandsons was planning to take his honeymoon before he got married: "People vary."

People do vary. And perspectives change. Today, for instance, more than 60 percent of first marriages are preceded by cohabitation, compared to virtually none just fifty years ago. For some couples, living together is simply better than being alone; for others, it is seen as a "try-out" marriage. Never mind the studies that point to the economic benefits of marriage or the evidence indicating that couples who live together before marriage are less likely to be happy together and more likely to get divorced.[2] To a lot of couples, living together—choosing the

---

2. Institute for American Values and University of Virginia National Marriage Project, "Social Indicators of Marital Health & Well-Being: Unmarried Cohabitation," http://stateofourunions.org/2010/si-cohabitation.php (accessed April 11, 2017).

(enjoyable) temporary over the (potentially rocky) permanent—
just makes sense.

Beth has three grown daughters. Two are married; the
youngest, Mariah, lives with her boyfriend, Henry, a fellow she
has been with for years. Mariah and Henry are both professing
Christians—"He was raised in the church," Beth exclaims. "His
mother even *worked* there!"—and they know that what they
are doing is (as she puts it) "not scriptural." And yet neither one
seems at all concerned about the spiritual or emotional ramifi-
cations of their choice. To them (and, in fact, to a majority of
their generation), cohabitation is a legitimate, even desirable,
alternative to marriage.

But Beth doesn't see it that way.

"I don't know what Henry's intentions are, and I don't want
my daughter to get hurt," Beth confides. "I have a journal full of
Bible verses I have prayed over their relationship—passages like
Romans 12:9, that they would hate what is evil and cling to what
is good; Hebrews 13:8–9, that they would not be carried away by
all kinds of strange teachings but have their hearts strengthened
by God's grace; and Colossians 1:9–14, that God would fill them
with the knowledge of his will and that they would please him in
every way. For the longest time, though, my main prayer was that
God would just help them realize that what they were doing was
wrong. They were sinning against God and against themselves,
and I wanted the Holy Spirit to *convict* them.

"And," she admits, "I told them so."

But then something happened. Beth had her journal open, ready to hear from God, and she sensed him speaking.

Stop talking.

Stop talking, God said. *They know. And nothing you can say or do will convince them to change. Instead of praying for the Holy Spirit to convict Mariah and Henry, pray that he will show them my love.*

That changed Beth's prayer strategy. She held on to many of the verses she'd been praying, but she layered other prayers on top of them, prayers for God to soften the couple's hearts, so that he could love them back into his kingdom and accomplish his best purposes for their lives, whether or not they were supposed to get married.[3]

================================

Prayer Principle

God's ways are not our ways. Ask him to show
you how to pray for your children.

================================

In adjusting both her perspective and her prayers, Beth found her own heart transformed. Even though nothing appears to have changed in how Mariah and Henry regard their living arrangement, she has peace. "God's ways are always better than my ways," she says, "and that includes knowing how to pray.

---

3. Beth's prayer verses include Ezekiel 36:26; Philippians 1:2–6; Romans 8:16; Malachi 3:6–7; 1 John 2:16–27; Romans 2:4.

Whenever I try to step into my kids' lives to make something happen, I just mess things up. But God always does it best."

The notion that God's ways are not our ways didn't originate with Beth—you can find that one in Isaiah 55—but it's something that every praying parent undoubtedly understands. Grace and her husband, Paul, met in college, and when their alma mater offered a soccer scholarship to their daughter, Lillie, they were thrilled. Two years into college, though, everything changed. A combination of injuries and academic issues sidelined their daughter, and when Lillie told them she was leaving school, Grace and Paul were not sure what to think. They agreed that college might not be the best fit for their girl, but most of their friends' children had college degrees; what would Lillie do with her life?

Prayer Principle

As your children navigate the path to adulthood, ask God to help them be wise and make the most of every opportunity.

Personable and attractive, Lillie moved home and quickly found work in a women's clothing store. "That's fine for now," Paul said, "but she can't keep living with us forever." Grace knew her husband was right—and that Lillie didn't *want* to live with her folks long-term either—but she wasn't sure how to pray. Years of driving soccer carpools and taking Lillie on college recruiting trips hadn't prepared her to be a career counselor, and she had no idea what her daughter should do or what the future held.

"Work in Lillie to will and to act according to your good purpose," she prayed. "And let her be wise, making the most of every opportunity and understanding your will for her life."[4]

In addition to working in the boutique, Lillie began volunteering with a high school youth group. One day, Lillie came home from work with a smile on her face. "The most beautiful woman came into the shop today," she said, "and we started talking. She's a makeup artist, and she gets all of these bookings for commercials and weddings. She offered to let me shadow her on a shoot she's doing next week."

"Does that mean you want to go to cosmetology school?" Paul asked.

"Maybe," Lillie answered. "At least I think so. I'm going to check it out."

Paul wasn't sure what he thought of Lillie's plan—he knew more people who had gone to business school than beauty school—but he didn't object. Instead, his chief concern was financial. "You gave up your soccer scholarship," he said, "and that was okay. But if you're going to go back to school, you'll need to figure out how to pay for it."

Lillie agreed, and together she and Paul worked on a budget that would allow her to afford to live on her own within six

---

4. Philippians 2:13; Ephesians 5:15–17.

months. She kept her job at the clothing shop and signed up for classes at a local cosmetology school. It was a schedule that, remarkably, still allowed her to spend some time with the youth group.

"She seems to be thriving," Grace says. "Lillie has always been a big encourager for other girls, whether it was on her soccer teams or in youth group. Now, she says she loves helping women discover how to make themselves as beautiful on the outside as they are on the inside.

"It's not a path we would have ever considered for our daughter, but it's obviously the right one. God is using her talents and her personality in ways we could have never imagined."

=================== *Prayer Principle* ===================

God gave your children unique talents and abilities.
Trust him to put these attributes to good use.

At the beginning of the chapter, I said that the pathway to adulthood is not as clear or as quick as it used to be. Many of today's young adults—our kids and their peers—are delaying marriage, putting off having children, and trying out a mix of work (including internships and part-time jobs) before settling into a career. Some may be plagued by what sociologists call "prolonged adolescence," but for a significant number of their generation, these choices have more to do with wanting to make a difference in the world—to live lives marked by purpose—than with being unfocused or lazy. And despite facing student debt or economic uncertainty, making money is not always a decision driver; more than 50 percent of millennials say they would take a pay cut to find work that matches their values, while 90 percent want to use their skills for good.[5]

My friend Elaine's son, Ben, fits this description perfectly. Unlike his parents (who graduated from college, got jobs, got married, bought a townhouse, and then had Ben and his brother), Ben and his wife are forgoing (at least for now) things like home ownership, child rearing, and stepping onto anything resembling a corporate ladder. Instead, they are using their skills—engineering degrees—to design and build bridges, roads, water filtration systems, and other critically needed projects in Cambodia.

"The kids knew before they even met each other that God wanted them to serve overseas," Elaine says. "They went to college to become engineers with that goal in mind. I know we won't see them for years at a time—and I already miss hugging them—but when my children graduated from college, I prayed that God would put them where he wanted them, and I asked that if it wasn't nearby, he'd give us the means to visit them. And he's been faithful."

---

5. Adam Smiley Poswolsky, "What Millennial Employees Really Want," *Fast Company*, June 4, 2015, www.fastcompany.com/3046989/what-millennial-employees -really-want (accessed April 11, 2017).

Elaine also told me about a verse, Proverbs 22:29, that God showed her for Ben when he was just fourteen years old. It's one she's been praying over her son's life ever since: "Do you see someone skilled in their work? They will serve before kings." Elaine doesn't know whether Ben will ever serve before an earthly king, but she knows that, in blessing her son as he goes off to the other side of the world, traveling a path to adulthood that looks nothing like her own, he is already serving the King.

Poised for Prayer

Our four children were all under ten years old when I wrote *Praying the Scriptures for Your Children*. I had no idea how their lives would take shape, but I included a section on praying for your child's purpose in life. Thinking about parents like the ones you've met in this chapter—parents whose kids are choosing unfamiliar or unexpected paths—I was reminded of something I wrote in that chapter: "As parents, it is deceptively easy to confuse our job with God's and to start nudging our kids toward a particular career or ministry opportunity."[6]

Now that my kids are grown, I might expand that statement. It is deceptively easy to confuse my job with God's and start nudging—pushing, even—them toward a particular career,

---

6. Jodie Berndt, *Praying the Scriptures for Your Children: Discover How to Pray God's Purpose for Their Lives* (Grand Rapids: Zondervan, 2001), 204.

ministry, apartment, neighborhood, marriage partner, investment, or parenting style.

And that's just for starters.

But there's a better way. Here's what else I wrote all those years ago (and for me, Jean Fleming's wise counsel means even more today than it did back then):

> Rather than pigeonholing or manipulating our kids into a life path that might not line up with God's design, let's learn to see our kids through God's eyes—and align ourselves with his plan for their lives. To this end, author Jean Fleming recommends regular times of prayer and planning for each child. As we bring our children before the Lord, she says we should:
>
> - *Acknowledge* God's hand on their lives, even before they were born.
> - *Admit* any areas we resent in the way God put our children together.
> - *Accept* God's design for each child, thanking him for how he or she is made.
> - *Affirm* God's purpose in creating our children for his glory.
> - *Ally* ourselves with God in his plans for their lives.[7]

---

7. Jean Fleming, *A Mother's Heart: A Look at Values, Vision, and Character for the Christian Mother* (Colorado Springs: NavPress, 1996), 89.

Of course, trusting God and his plan for our kids—along with accepting his timetable—is not always easy. But if we remember that he loves them (even more than we do) and that he promises to work in all things for the good of those who love him,[8] we can quit pushing and prodding—and get down to the real business of praying.[9]

Good advice. And now as I pray for the children who have left my nest but not my heart, I just need to remember it.

---

8. Romans 8:28.
9. Berndt, *Praying the Scriptures for Your Children*, 209.

Prayers You Can Use

For Yourself

Heavenly Father . . .

Show me how to align my prayers with your plans for my children, since if we ask anything according to your will, you have promised to hear us.   1 JOHN 5:14

When my child's transition to adulthood doesn't look like I thought it would, help me to trust that your thoughts and your ways are higher and better than mine.

ISAIAH 55:8–9

When you do something new or different in my child's life, give me eyes to perceive it. Don't let me get hung up on the past (the way we've "always done it"), but let me honor you as you make a way for my child in the wilderness of adulthood.   ISAIAH 43:18–19

For Your Children

Heavenly Father . . .

Do not let _____ worry that people will look down on him because he is young. Instead, may he set an example for other believers in speech, in conduct, in love, in faith, and in purity.   1 TIMOTHY 4:12

Take out _____'s stony, stubborn heart and give her a tender, responsive heart. Put your Spirit in her, so that she will follow your decrees and be careful to obey you.

EZEKIEL 36:26–27 NLT

Instruct _____ and teach him in the way he should go; counsel him with your loving eye on him. PSALM 32:8

No matter what _____ is planning (for her career, marriage, or anything else), may it be your purpose that prevails.   PROVERBS 19:21

As _____ moves into a new job or neighborhood, may he be alert to opportunities to serve you by offering food, clothing, and caring friendship to people in need.

MATTHEW 25:35–40

Cause _____ to be careful how she lives. Let her be wise, make the most of every opportunity, and understand your will. EPHESIANS 5:15–17

May _____ be trustworthy in how he handles wealth, and single-minded in his devotion to serving you.

LUKE 16:10–13

Fulfill your purpose for _____; do not abandon the works of your hands. PSALM 138:8

Thank you that you created _____ to do good works; lead her into those things that you have prepared in advance for her to do. EPHESIANS 2:10

Don't let _____ look down on other believers or criticize them, since he will one day give an account of himself to you. ROMANS 14:10–12

Prompt _____ to seek you as she makes decisions about marriage, family, and career, since you know how she is wired ("woven together") and what her future holds.

PSALM 139:15–16

As _____ reaches adulthood, may he put childishness behind him and learn to think, speak, and reason like a man. 1 CORINTHIANS 13:11

CHAPTER 4

A Year of Prayer

Be joyful in hope, patient in
affliction, faithful in prayer.

ROMANS 12:12

In 1999, my friend Margaret and I attended the fifteenth anniversary celebration for Moms in Prayer.[1] We each had four children, and we were eager to learn more about how we could pray for them. Being surrounded by hundreds of other praying mothers, all of whom had stories to tell about God's faithfulness to their families, was beyond encouraging, and Margaret and I came away with a renewed vision for the power of prayer.

One idea we picked up was to make "prayer hands" that we could use to pray one particular verse for each child all year long. We spent some time thinking and praying about where each one of our children was (spiritually, as well as socially, physically, and emotionally), and we asked God to show us how he wanted to work in their lives during the year ahead. Then we selected

---

1. Moms in Prayer has passed the thirty-year mark now; get more information on this international organization at www.MomsInPrayer.org.

a Bible verse that spoke to that need, and we turned it into a personalized prayer (the way you've done with the prayers at the end of each chapter in this book). We traced each child's hand onto a piece of colored paper, wrote the prayer and the date on the hand, cut it out, and stuck it on the refrigerator (because what house with four kids under age ten doesn't have some sort of hand art on the refrigerator?).

Today, nearly twenty years later, I no longer put the hands on the refrigerator (because what house with four kids over age twenty has hand art on the refrigerator?), but I keep the current requests in my prayer journal. And I started making bookmarks instead of hands when our two oldest girls got married, since I didn't think my sons-in-law would want me tracing their hands (and since their giant man-hands would not have fit in my prayer journal anyway). I keep the whole collection in a big Ziploc bag. It's one of those things I'd grab if the house ever caught on fire.

I love the spiritual story these paper hands tell and the way they provide a tangible record of God's handiwork. By devoting a whole year to praying for one particular need or concern, I could relax (well, sort of) and wait on God's timing. And as I watched his faithfulness and provision take root in my children's lives, I found my own faith deepening as well, to the point where I could really believe that "he who began a good work" in them "will bring it to completion at the day of Jesus Christ."[2]

---

2. Philippians 1:6 ESV.

Prayer Principle

Choosing one verse to pray all year long expands
your time horizon and allows an awareness of God's
faithfulness to take root in your prayer life.

If you like this idea of praying about one key need over a
long period of time, consider making prayer hands (perhaps for
your grandchildren, if you've hit that season) or bookmarks of
your own. Don't get hung up on having to pick the "perfect"
verse (there aren't any bad ones); just choose something that fits.

Here's an example. In 2001, Robbie was a kindergartner. The
fact that he was our first (and only) boy did little to console us
when he became our first (and only) child to wind up in the principal's office. We knew he was more interested in sports than he
was in books; what we didn't expect was that he'd be willing and
able to hit just about anything—a baseball or a classmate—with
surprising dexterity. After a series of depressing parent-teacher
conferences, I was ready to buy my son his first pack of cigarettes
and let him loose on a street corner, since I figured he'd wind
up there anyway.

That was the year I turned to Proverbs 23:23–24 for help.
Here's what I wrote on his prayer hand: *Help Robbie to get wisdom, discipline, and understanding. Let him be the righteous man
who brings joy to his parents, the wise son in whom we delight.*

As the months went by, we began to notice little changes at

home (Robbie's sisters, for example, stopped flinching when he walked by), but I wasn't prepared for what I saw on the teacher's report at the next conference. Reading upside down, I could see what looked like a big, fat zero right next to the word "Behavior." I wanted to cry. But then the teacher flipped the paper around. She told me she'd been blown away by the turnaround in Robbie's classroom conduct: "I gave him an *O* for Outstanding," she said. "He's really become a bright spot in the class."

I did start to cry then. And I'd cry even more right now if I took the time to write out all the ways that God has answered that Proverbs 23 prayer in my son's life. It hasn't been a spotless journey from anger to self-control (a few of our friends still love to tell the story of when he got ejected from a lacrosse game as a nine-year-old), but it has been an incredible one. Robbie has truly become a righteous man who brings joy to his parents. And it's not because of anything we did (I was the one with the cigarette plan, remember?). It is all because of God's faithfulness.

In 2003, Virginia was a first-grader who had a lot of enthusiasm for Jesus. So much so that when she overheard another child talking about God—saying that her family didn't believe in Jesus and that they thought prayer was stupid—she stopped in her tracks. "She doesn't believe in Jesus?" Virginia asked, to nobody in particular, but loud enough for half the kids on the playground to hear. "She thinks praying is *stupid*?"

And then, before anyone could answer, Virginia pronounced her judgment: "Well, *she's* going to hell!"

When Hillary, who had witnessed the scene, told us the story that night, I cringed. (Wouldn't you?) I loved Virginia's boldness, but I knew God had to temper it with a measure of grace if she was ever going to be able to share her faith effectively (or if she was ever going to have any friends!). I asked God to smooth her rough edges and fill her heart with wisdom and understanding, not dampening her spiritual zeal, but clothing it with mercy.

I used a concordance to look up verses about wisdom, and I found a beautiful promise in Daniel 12:3. Here's what I wrote on Virginia's hand that year: *I pray that Virginia would be wise, shining like the brightness of the heavens, and that she would lead many to righteousness, and thereby shine like the stars for ever and ever.*

Here again, God proved himself—that year, and even more in the years that followed. Today, as a young adult in the corporate world, Virginia is as happy on a barstool as she is in a Bible study, but in both places she is eager to hear people's stories and gently point them toward Christ. She still blurts stuff out from time to time (she's her mother's daughter), but God is shaping her and using her to scatter the darkness—and all I can do is look at the Lord and say, "Thank you."

Lest you think all of my yearlong prayers are so dramatic or that I'm particularly sensitive to my family's deepest spiritual needs, I'll be honest and tell you that there are times when my choice of a prayer verse has been sparked by something as trivial as a new habit or hobby. When my husband, for instance, graduated to reading glasses and began telling me about his post-tennis aches and pains, I drew inspiration from Psalm 92: *May Robbie still bear fruit in his old age and always stay fresh and green.*[3]

(And just so you know, Robbie didn't love that choice at first. But he came around. Because he's a smart guy. And who wouldn't want to stay fresh and green?)

Perhaps the most surprising annual prayer verse (at least to me) was the one I prayed for Hillary in 2014. I was doing one of those "Read through the Bible in Two Years" plans, and when December rolled around, I found myself in Isaiah. I'd been asking God to show me what I should pray for Hillary. When I came upon Isaiah 62:1–5, I had the strongest impression that it applied to my girl. But it was a longish passage—too long to fit on a hand—so I dismissed it. Plus, it talked about no longer being called "Deserted" or "Desolate," but being called by a new name. I knew Hillary had been wrestling with some anxiety and insecurity, but I didn't think things were *that* bad. Like, she didn't seem *desolate*.

But I kept coming back to the verses, and finally, out of a compelling sense that they were right for her, I condensed them like this: *May Hillary be called by a new name. May she be a crown of beauty in the Lord's hand, a royal diadem in the hand of God.*

My first clue that God might be up to something—and that this verse really might be a good one for Hillary—was when I looked up the word *diadem*. I had sung it in church ("Bring forth

---

3. Psalm 92:12–14.

the royal di-a-dem!"), but I had no idea what one actually was. I figured it was some sort of sparkly tiara, since it sounded like "diamond," but I Googled the word to be sure.

A diadem is, in fact, a crown. But as it turns out, it's also the name of a software—DIAdem—that is "specifically designed to help engineers and scientists quickly locate, inspect, analyze, and report on measurement data using one software tool."[4] Hillary, as it happens, is a rocket scientist. Truly. I don't have any idea what she actually does at work, but I'd bet my English major there's a fair amount of locating, inspecting, analyzing, and reporting on measurement data going on. If God had plans to make her a "royal diadem," that could only mean good things for her job.

Not only that, but if Hillary was feeling anxious or insecure in any way, I took the Isaiah 62 verse to mean that God was going to change that. In his capable hands, she would *know* she was a "crown of beauty." She wouldn't be deserted or desolate; she'd get a new name: verse 4 said she'd be called "Hephzibah" and "Beulah."

This time, I didn't have to Google because my Bible translated the names in the footnotes: Hephzibah means *my delight is in her*. Beulah means *married*.

Haha. I thought that was funny. If anybody was going to be called "Beulah" in our house, it would be Annesley, who had been dating her boyfriend, Geoff, for nearly six years, since

4. National Instruments, "NI DIAdem," www.ni.com/diadem (accessed April 11, 2017).

their high school prom. Hillary had only been hanging out with Charlie for a few months; I didn't even know if they were serious. God could delight in Hillary all he wanted, but calling her Beulah? That was a good one.

You can guess what happened.

Geoff asked Annesley to marry him, and we started planning a wedding. And then, before we'd even finished picking table-cloths for their reception (a selection process that, as it turns out, is more complex than you might imagine), Charlie pulled out a ring! Like Geoff, he'd gotten Robbie's blessing on the proposal, but Hillary was totally surprised—as was I. Looking back, I should have known God had something up his sleeve: When you tell a mama to pray that her girl will get a new name, you don't mess around. Annesley may have had a head start on the tablecloths, but four months after she walked down the aisle, Hillary was Beulah too.

=== *Prayer Principle* ===

When God gives you a promise to pray for your adult child, leave room for him to fulfill it in ways that go beyond anything you could have imagined.

In her book *Live a Praying Life*, Jennifer Kennedy Dean makes the case that the starting place for understanding how prayer works is to recognize the sovereignty of God. "Nothing takes him by surprise," she writes. "He is never making things up as He goes along. He is never confronted with a situation He had not expected and planned for and woven into His sovereign and redemptive plan."[5]

We may *think* we are suggesting a plan or even changing God's mind when we pray, but in reality, *he* is the initiator. He gives us a glimpse into what he is doing in order to awaken in us some sort of response or action or prayer—one he had *expected* to awaken.

In other words, God knew he had plans to give Hillary a new name—not just moving her from a place of insecurity ("Deserted") to one of peace ("My Delight"), but also giving her a literal new name, moving her from Berndt to Blakeley. He'd already woven those things into his sovereign plan for her life, and he gave me the privilege, as her mother, of praying them into being.

You can pick up a book like this, flip to the back of a chapter, and find a dozen God-breathed prayers for your child. There is nothing wrong with that. But if we want to fully experience what Jesus meant in John 15:7 when he said, "If you remain in me and my words remain in you, ask whatever you wish, and it will be done for you," we need to read the Bible for ourselves. We need to allow God's message to *dwell* in our minds, shaping our desires and giving voice to our prayers.

---

5. Jennifer Kennedy Dean, *Live a Praying Life* (Birmingham, AL: New Hope, 2010), 22.

When it comes to reading the Bible—regularly, and in such a way that it can transform our perspective—it can help to have a system. There are all sorts of programs you can access online; you'll find a variety of options at Bible Gateway (www .biblegateway.com/reading-plans). My personal favorite is probably "The Bible in One Year." This reading plan features daily excerpts from both the Old and New Testaments, and it comes with insightful commentary to help you apply God's Word to your everyday life. If you're like me and you love the idea of waking up with a plan, get The Bible in One Year delivered to your email in-box or download the app at www .bibleinoneyear.org.

And take it from me: Don't worry if it takes you a few tries to get started. Just choose an approach that works for you (I have one friend who spent a whole year just reading the psalms!). And if you miss a day or two (or a whole week or two), don't quit. Don't ever quit. Just get back in the saddle. Because here's the thing: the more you read God's Word, the more you'll know it, and the more you know it, the more you'll love it—and the more it will define and empower your prayers.

Prayer Principle

Reading the Bible allows God's message to penetrate our minds, shape our desires, and give voice to our prayers.

Poised for Prayer

Linking your Bible reading to your prayer life makes them both more exciting. When you read Scripture with an eye toward discovering prayer prompts, God will often make a particular passage or promise come alive. It's like walking along the seashore looking for shells and suddenly seeing one that captivates you in a way you had not expected. You cannot help but pick it up! In the same way, you will be reading along (like I was in Isaiah), and you'll happen upon a particular verse, tucked in among all the others on the page, and you will just *know* its message is for you. It will be the very thing you needed that day or in that season. And so you'll pick it up; you will take it to heart. You'll be excited to make it your prayer.

I'm going to close this chapter, not with *prayer* verses, but with *promise* verses—verses that showcase the beauty, reliability, and transformational power of God's Word. Ultimately, the time we spend reading the Bible and praying the Scriptures isn't just about pulling favor and blessings into the lives of our loved ones; it's also about shaping our own lives—drawing *us* closer to Christ, letting him lead us, asking him (as the disciples did) to "teach us to pray."[6]

It's about letting God work in us, even as we ask him to work in the lives of our children.

---

6. Luke 11:1.

Promises You Can Use

If you abide in me, and my words abide in you, ask whatever you wish, and it will be done for you. By this my Father is glorified, that you bear much fruit and so prove to be my disciples.   JOHN 15:7–8 ESV

For the word of God is alive and active. Sharper than any double-edged sword, it penetrates even to dividing soul and spirit, joints and marrow; it judges the thoughts and attitudes of the heart.   HEBREWS 4:12

All Scripture is God-breathed and is useful for teaching, rebuking, correcting and training in righteousness.

2 TIMOTHY 3:16

Keep this Book of the Law always on your lips; meditate on it day and night, so that you may be careful to do everything written in it. Then you will be prosperous and successful.

JOSHUA 1:8

The grass withers and the flowers fall, but the word of our God endures forever.   ISAIAH 40:8

I gain understanding from your precepts; therefore I hate every wrong path. Your word is a lamp for my feet, a light on my path.   PSALM 119:104–5

I have hidden your word in my heart that I might not sin against you.   PSALM 119:11

Let the word of Christ dwell in you richly, teaching and admonishing one another in all wisdom, singing psalms and hymns and spiritual songs, with thankfulness in your hearts to God.   COLOSSIANS 3:16 ESV

For everything that was written in the past was written to teach us, so that through the endurance taught in the Scriptures and the encouragement they provide we might have hope.   ROMANS 15:4

Praise be to the LORD, who has given rest to his people Israel just as he promised. Not one word has failed of all the good promises he gave through his servant Moses.
                              1 KINGS 8:56

Jesus answered, "It is written: 'Man shall not live on bread alone, but on every word that comes from the mouth of God.'"   MATTHEW 4:4

As the rain and the snow come down from heaven, and do not return to it without watering the earth and making it bud and flourish . . . so is my word that goes out from my mouth: It will not return to me empty, but will accomplish what I desire and achieve the purpose for which I sent it.

ISAIAH 55:10–11

PART 2

PRAYING
for Your
ADULT CHILD'S
Relationships

CHAPTER 5

Praying for Good Friends and Fellowship

As iron sharpens iron,
so one person sharpens another.

PROVERBS 27:17

"*Fellowship*," writes John Ortberg, "has become a churchy word that suggests basements and red punch and awkward conversation. But it is really a word for the flow of rivers of living water between one person and another, and we cannot live without it."[1]

We cannot live without it. I get that. We moved around a lot when our kids were growing up, and every time they went off to a new school, my first prayers were for them to find life-giving friendships, the kind marked by things like loyalty, joy, and a vibrant commitment to Christ. That didn't change when they went off to colleges and jobs. In fact, I remember the high school counselor asking Robbie and me what we were looking for in a college

---

1. John Ortberg, *The Me I Want to Be: Becoming God's Best Version of You* (Grand Rapids: Zondervan, 2010), 182.

for Hillary, our eldest. He expected, I guess, for us to say something like "affordable tuition" or "strong academic reputation" or even something lofty, like "opportunities to pursue bio-medical research." I think the guy was a little stunned when I told him my answer: I wanted my daughter to go someplace where she could make good friends and enjoy strong Christian fellowship.

And now that our children have moved into adulthood—into a world of new cities, new marriages, and new jobs—I am asking God for the same thing. They may have a thousand contacts in their phones or on their social media accounts, but those aren't the same thing as *connections*, and I am convinced that (to borrow a phrase from Ortberg) we are "designed to flourish in connectedness."[2] The happiest people are not those who have the most money or the best looks or the highest IQ. "What distinguishes consistently happier people from less happy people," writes Ortberg, "is the presence of rich, deep, joy-producing, life-changing, meaningful relationships."[3]

God has answered those friendship prayers, but the road to connectedness has not always been easy. I remember dropping Hillary off at college, where someone had chalked on the sidewalk, "WELCOME TO THE BEST FOUR YEARS OF YOUR LIFE!" The words held such promise, but two months later, as the newness wore off and homesickness set in, they seemed almost hollow. Even though she had a great roommate

---

2. Ibid., 186.
3. Ibid., 182–83.

and her life swirled with classes and social activities, Hillary had not yet found "her people," and that hurt.

Maybe every kid who moves away from home for college or a job goes through that. My friend Allison has a daughter, Emily, who intentionally chose a small private school over the big state university because it had a religious affiliation and she thought it would be easy to find friends there who shared her Christian faith.

========== *Prayer Principle* ==========

We are created for connection. Ask God to bless your child with rich and meaningful relationships.

Emily's freshman year started well. She loved her classes and professors, and she quickly bonded with some girls in her dorm. One by one, though, these gals found themselves drawn into the school's party culture, and Emily began to feel increasingly isolated and alone. By the time she came home for spring break, she seemed to be a different person; her upbeat, cheerful demeanor had been replaced by something more akin to depression.

Allison wasn't sure just how to pray, but the words "rescue her" kept coming to her mind, along with the promise she found in Psalm 34:7: "The angel of the LORD encamps around those who fear him, and he delivers them."

Allison began asking God to "camp" around Emily, letting

her sense his nearness in her life. Using the psalm as a prompt, Allison prayed that God would deliver her *from* things like loneliness, depression, and worry—even as he delivered her *to* people whose company she would enjoy, young women whose conversations were "full of grace" and "seasoned with salt."[4]

Things got worse before they got better. Emily loved the education she was getting, but she just didn't know how much longer she could go on, surrounded by people with whom she seemed to have so little in common. She began to think she should transfer.

The problem was that Emily felt like God wanted her to stay put. She didn't know what he had in store but, out of obedience more than desire, she returned for her sophomore year. She had heard that the college had a club lacrosse team, and since she had played in high school, she figured she would give it a try. If nothing else, at least she'd meet some people who shared her interest in the sport.

There she met three young women who—to Emily's amazement—turned out to be believers. "We've been talking about starting a Bible study," one of them said, "but we don't have anyone who can lead it." A few nights later, Emily attended a dinner where she met a professor who confided that she had been asking God to give her a group of female students she could lead in a Bible study. Emily could hardly believe her ears! The girls began meeting with the older woman, and for the first time since she'd

---

4. Colossians 4:6.

enrolled in the school, Emily felt like she belonged. God had used her love for a sport to deliver the blessing of genuine fellowship.

Perhaps even harder than making new friends in college is the challenge of making them in professional life. Not only is the pool of prospects often much smaller, but busy work schedules can leave less time for cultivating and nourishing relationships.

===== *Prayer Principle* =====

Ask God to use your children's worldly interests to connect them to people whose passion is for him.

Sylvia's daughter, Hayley, works for an event-planning company that puts on major fund-raisers all over the country, from early-morning road races to glitzy evening galas. Most of Hayley's coworkers are "work hard, play hard" types. At first, she was captivated by the fast-paced lifestyle, but now, two years into her job, she is just tired. Being in a new city and working with different teams of people almost every weekend make it hard for her to build meaningful relationships, and the novelty of going out for drinks after the workday is over has lost its allure. Hayley still enjoys the logistics of planning—and the satisfaction of seeing an event come together—but she longs for a sense of community and connection in her personal life.

I had a job that required a lot of travel when I was Hayley's age. I remember how much I enjoyed the weekends when I was home—not just because I could sleep in my own bed, but also because I loved my Sunday school class, which was geared toward young professionals. In addition to the teaching we got on Sunday mornings, the group often met for cookouts or volleyball games on the beach on Saturdays, plus occasional midweek events. It was a great way to meet people and make friends.

"Does Hayley go to church?" I asked Sylvia.

"She does when she's in town," Sylvia said. "But they have this approach to small groups that they think will appeal to young adults. You do a group for six weeks, and then it's over, and they mix it up and you start something else with a whole new group. I guess they want to make it easy on a generation that seems averse to commitment, but it doesn't seem like six weeks is long enough to really get to know people or forge lasting friendships."

I was, honestly, impressed that Hayley was trying to plug in at a church. I'd read the articles—the ones that tell how millennials are "leaving the church in droves," and how 80 percent of kids raised in the church will be "disengaged" by the time they are twenty-nine[5]—and the findings ran parallel to the conversations I had with quite a few parents whose adult children are not (at least currently) going to church.

"My son has two jobs right now," one mother confided. "Sunday mornings are one of the only times he can rest during the week."

5. Preston Sprinkle, "Why Are Millennials Leaving the Church in Droves? Part 1," September 16, 2015, www.patheos.com/blogs/theologyintheraw/2015/09/why-are-millennials-leaving-the-church-in-droves-part-1 (accessed April 11, 2017).

"My daughter works in retail, and Sunday is a big day for her," said another.

"I think my daughter would get involved in a church if she had someone to go with," one father said. "But none of her friends go to church, and it's no fun to go alone."

(That one hit home with me; I wouldn't like going to church alone either.)

=============== *Prayer Principle* ===============

If your child is not going to church, ask God
to prompt someone to invite him.

Perhaps the reason I heard most often for not getting involved in a church is that—according to several young people who'd been raised in the church and quit going—"I don't need a church to have a relationship with God."

I was mulling that one over (and thinking of all the reasons we *should* go to church, from the Hebrews 10:25 command ["not giving up meeting together"] to the fact that we really do flourish—spiritually as well as socially—in Christian community), when I got an email from my friend Helen.

Helen's daughter, Jane, moved to Los Angeles a year ago. A lifelong churchgoer, Jane knew she wanted to find a church home in L.A., but she struggled to find a place where she felt like she belonged. One church was too much like a rock concert

("They had concessions and fog machines," Jane told her mom, "and my seat literally shook when the music started"); the next one she tried was "just too boring." I knew Helen had been praying that her daughter would discover a place to connect, and I was glad when she told me Jane had finally found a good fit.

And I was thrilled—and given all the gloomy research about her generation's churchgoing habits, a little surprised—when Helen shared an excerpt from one of Jane's emails:

> It has also just been awesome to watch everyone actually want to go to church, so much more than in college. Boys and girls. People are just realizing that we are not in college and just have to find comfort/joy/consistency/ identity somewhere and everyone is reverting back to going to church. I'm trying so hard to get people there and I've met some really, really cool people who aren't there yet but will be!

Wow. There's one millennial who's bucking the trend, and from the tone of her email, it sounds like a lot of her peers are bucking it with her.

I loved what Jane wrote about needing to find comfort, joy, consistency, and identity. That's what my kids are looking for too, both in their earthly friendships and in their relationship with God. The pollsters may paint a bleak picture of young adults leaving the church, and our kids may struggle with a sense of isolation at school or in their jobs, but the fact that they *want* things like comfort and consistency gives me hope. They are craving genuine connection—*which is the very thing God longs to provide*!

Poised for Prayer

Matthew Lieberman, a Harvard-trained psychologist who is one of the world's leading authorities on social neuroscience, would understand this craving for connection. He says that the human brain is wired to be social. "Love and belonging might seem like a convenience we can live without," he writes, "but our biology is built to thirst for connection because it is linked to our most basic survival needs."[6] In layman's terms, I guess what the doctor is saying is that we desire and need friends as much as we want (and have to have) chocolate.

(Or maybe chicken. But you get the idea.)

Our kids need good friends. And as we pray for God to satisfy this hunger, let's look to the Scriptures for insight on what matters most. There are, obviously, all sorts of good things we could ask God for; here are three of my top requests:

Let's pray for *constancy*. The Bible offers several portraits of friendships marked by loyalty, dependability, and faithfulness. Jonathan became "one in spirit" with David, giving him his robe

---

6. Matthew D. Lieberman, *Social: Why Our Brains are Wired to Connect* (New York: Crown, 2013), 43.

(symbolic of his identity) and making a covenant of friendship that would last between their descendants forever.[7] Ruth chose to stay with her mother-in-law after the death of her husband, even though it meant leaving her family, her home, and her country. "Your people will be my people," she vowed, "and your God my God."[8] And, of course, we have the ultimate example of constancy in Jesus, who promised to be with us "always, to the very end of the age."[9] Let's ask God to give our kids faithful friends and to draw them into a life-giving relationship with Jesus, the one who gave up his life "for his friends."[10]

Let's pray for *transparency* too. Susan and Barbie are two of my oldest and dearest friends. We roomed together in college, where we gave each other permission to be brutally honest. It didn't matter if we were critiquing an iffy outfit or confronting each other about a questionable behavior; we spoke the truth. We tried to do so with love, but even the gentlest rebukes sometimes hurt. "Faithful," the Bible says, "are the wounds of a friend."[11] Let's ask God to give our adult children friends like that—friends with whom they can admit their mistakes and find restoration, forgiveness, and genuine love.[12]

Finally, let's pray that our children will enjoy friendship

---

7. See 1 Samuel 18–20.
8. Ruth 1:16.
9. Matthew 28:20.
10. John 15:13 ESV.
11. Proverbs 27:6 ESV.
12. James 5:16; Ephesians 4:32.

with other believers, the "fellowship of the Holy Spirit"[13] that brings connection not just on the natural level, but also in the deepest recesses of the soul. Friendships forged around common interests (new babies, sports teams, good books) are wonderful, but when the common ground of eternity comes into play, the most satisfying relationships—the kind that transcend things like race, age, and socioeconomic background—can take root. Let's ask God to plant our kids in a vibrant church home and surround them with companions who will "spur them on toward love and good deeds" and run alongside them as they "pursue righteousness, faith, love and peace."[14]

And one more thing. Let's ask God to give *us* friends like that too, particularly as we pray for our children.

The Bible has a lot to say about the power that is unleashed when believers come together to pray. I've already mentioned Moses and his pals; the same sort of thing happened to Daniel. Tasked with the impossible (identifying and interpreting the king's dream), Daniel called his friends together to pray—and the mystery was revealed.[15] These examples (and plenty more) illustrate the prayer principle outlined in Matthew 18:19–20: "If two of you on earth agree about anything they ask for, it will be done for them by my Father in heaven. For where two or three gather in my name, there am I with them." Jesus is talking

---

13. 2 Corinthians 13:14.
14. Hebrews 10:24; 2 Timothy 2:22.
15. Daniel 2:17–19.

about rectifying offenses within the church in this passage, but the underlying concept—that authority is expressed in unity—manifests itself whenever believers gather to pray. This is, writes bestselling author Ray Stedman, "the charter principle underlying all prayer meetings!"[16]

If your spouse is not comfortable praying with you, or if you don't already have a friend who will join you in praying for your child, ask God to give you a prayer partner. Or two. Be alert to the names he might put on your heart, and don't be afraid to take the initiative and invite people to pray with you. You don't have to be formal or fancy; just jump in. (If you aren't sure where to begin, you can simply work your way through the verses in this book, picking one or two topics each week and praying them together.)

When your child moves away from home, he or she isn't the only one who's going to want friends. You're going to want a few too—and God knows just how to get you connected.

---

16. Ray C. Stedman, *Talking with My Father* (Grand Rapids: Discovery House, 1997), 101.

Prayers You Can Use

For Yourself

Heavenly Father...

Give me praying friends like Daniel had, and companions who will hold up my hands when I feel too weak or weary to pray, the way Aaron and Hur did for Moses.

DANIEL 2:17–29; EXODUS 17:15–16

As I pray for my child to find friends and fellowship, help me remember that you have promised never to leave us or forsake us. Thank you for being our friend.

HEBREWS 13:5

Show me how to point my child toward you, the friend who sticks closer than a brother.   PROVERBS 18:24

For Your Children

Heavenly Father...

Bless _____ with friends who will sharpen him as iron sharpens iron.   PROVERBS 27:17

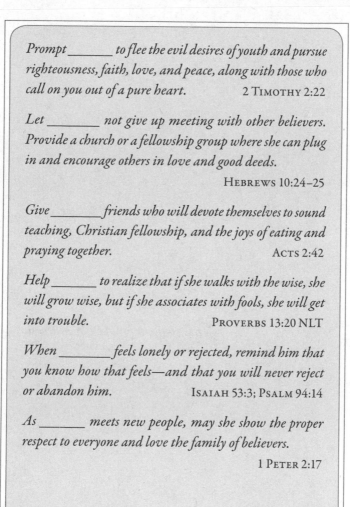

Prompt _____ to flee the evil desires of youth and pursue righteousness, faith, love, and peace, along with those who call on you out of a pure heart. 2 TIMOTHY 2:22

Let _____ not give up meeting with other believers. Provide a church or a fellowship group where she can plug in and encourage others in love and good deeds.

HEBREWS 10:24–25

Give _____ friends who will devote themselves to sound teaching, Christian fellowship, and the joys of eating and praying together. ACTS 2:42

Help _____ to realize that if she walks with the wise, she will grow wise, but if she associates with fools, she will get into trouble. PROVERBS 13:20 NLT

When _____ feels lonely or rejected, remind him that you know how that feels—and that you will never reject or abandon him. ISAIAH 53:3; PSALM 94:14

As _____ meets new people, may she show the proper respect to everyone and love the family of believers.

1 PETER 2:17

May _____ and his friends love one another in a way that shows other people that they are your disciples.

JOHN 13:35

Give _____ friends with whom she can be honest, even when it comes to confessing sin. And make _____ and her friends quick to forgive one another.

JAMES 5:16; EPHESIANS 4:32

Surround _____ with a community of believers who will carry each other's burdens.   GALATIANS 6:2

Thank you for laying down your life for _____. Call him your friend, and make known to him everything you have learned from your Father.   JOHN 15:13–15

May _____ walk in the light and enjoy fellowship with other believers.   1 JOHN 1:7

CHAPTER 6

Praying for a Future Spouse

*"Let her be the one the LORD has
chosen for my master's son."*

GENESIS 24:44

When the time came for his son to get married, Abraham had one main request: Isaac's bride couldn't be a Canaanite; rather, he wanted her to be someone from his own country. He sent his servant off to do the picking, and when the fellow got to Abraham's hometown, he prayed a very specific prayer: "LORD . . . make me successful today . . . May it be that when I say to a young woman, 'Please let down your jar that I may have a drink,' and she says, 'Drink, and I'll water your camels too'—let her be the one you have chosen for your servant Isaac."[1]

And that's exactly what happened. Rebekah showed up, gave the servant a drink, and then offered to fetch water for the camels

---

1. Genesis 24:12, 14.

too—all *ten* of them. Watching the girl run back and forth from the well (can you imagine?), the servant had to have known she was a keeper: hardworking, thoughtful, generous, patient, and strong. Throw in the fact that she was a looker and a virgin from Abraham's very own family, and the servant literally pulled out the ring.

(It was a nose ring. But still.)

While most modern-day parents don't have a servant to do our spouse shopping, many of us are like Abraham when it comes to having a wish list about the person our children will marry. I did a little informal survey for this chapter, and the list of must-haves was fascinating. I spoke to parents who hope their kids will marry someone who is intelligent, emotionally stable, good-looking, or from an intact home. Some moms and dads want their children to find their mates early (both to enjoy the blessing of marriage and to lessen the pressures of sexual temptation during the adult years); others hope their kids will wait until they have carved their own niche and grown mature enough to make wise decisions. I heard from parents who want athletes, people with a sense of humor, or (my personal favorite) "tan-able skin" so that when the grandbabies come along, the grandparents won't have to worry about them getting sunburned when they babysit.

And almost everyone I talked to said they wanted their son or daughter to marry a Christian.

Fern Nichols, who started the Moms in Prayer organization,

says she used 2 Corinthians 6:14 as she prayed for her son's eventual wife. Ty loved girls (and they loved him back), but Fern didn't want him "yoked together" with an unbeliever, since (as the Bible puts it) "what fellowship can light have with darkness?"[2]

The way Fern tells it, Ty would "bring home a little sweetie, cute as she could be, who didn't love Jesus. So I would love her, pray for her salvation, invite her to dinner, and then 'pray her out'!" Fern figured that God knew whether or not the little sweetie was going to accept him as Lord and Savior, so she concentrated on loving the gal and praying for her and simply asked God to "remove her" if she wasn't the right one. And when The One finally did show up—a Kentucky girl who reminded Fern of Anne of Green Gables—Fern watched her for a couple of weeks and then said, "Lord, I think I could handle her in our family." Nine months later, Ty and Patti were married.[3]

And then there's my friend Brigitte. Like Fern, she prayed that her children would marry believers—but she thought it would be good if they also came from a similar background so that they'd have the same sort of family traditions and culture. "And so," she laughs, "my son went out and married a Persian who could barely speak English!"

Brigitte adores her daughter-in-law. But the match took her

2. 2 Corinthians 6:14.
3. Fern Nichols, *Every Child Needs a Praying Mom* (Grand Rapids: Zondervan, 2003), 43–44.

by surprise ("No eye has seen, no ear has heard, no human mind has conceived what God has prepared for those who love him," she says),[4] and her experience dovetails with what I've heard from dozens of praying parents: *the person my child fell in love with and married is not the person I would have asked for or imagined.*

=========== *Prayer Principle* ===========

When you pray for your child's marriage partner, it's okay to be specific, but be prepared for God to surprise you.

Sandy and Pete began praying for their children's eventual mates the moment Abby and Brian were born. They wanted their children to grow up loving the Lord with their whole heart—and to marry people who felt the same way. That was tops on their list, but they had other requests. Sandy and Pete added other things to the list: They wanted in-laws who laughed easily and exhibited humility. They wanted mates who would mesh with and strengthen their family, the way that individual Christians build up the family of Christ. And they wanted athletes. A potential spouse didn't have to be an Olympic champion, but he or she had to at least be willing to go outside and throw a Frisbee.

Abby's husband came along first. He was everything on the list and then some. A strong Christian who knew his Bible almost

---

4. 1 Corinthians 2:9.

as well as he knew his own name, Matt was quick to challenge Pete to a tennis match or suggest a family pickup basketball game after dinner. Sandy and Pete were in heaven, and they looked forward to one day welcoming Brian's wife into the fold. That way, the teams would be even.

But Brian took his time. He dated a handful of girls, one or two of whom Sandy and Pete really liked, but nothing lasted. And when back-to-back breakups left his heart in tatters, Sandy realized that her son, at age thirty-one, still had some growing up to do.

Then along came Kendra. She was beautiful, rich, and from a large Christian family. And Brian was smitten.

Sandy and Pete weren't so sure. They'd been praying Proverbs 19:14 and asking God to provide a "prudent wife" for their son (which, to Sandy, meant someone sensible, wise, and discreet). Kendra was anything but. She was headstrong, vocal, and almost a whole decade younger than Brian (and to Sandy's maternal eye, Kendra's youthful clothing looked more alluring than discreet). She couldn't blame Brian for noticing Kendra's charms, but she was not at all certain that the infatuation was wise.

But it was certainly mutual, and just a few months into the relationship, Brian announced that he was going to ask Kendra to marry him. Her parents were enthusiastic about the idea, as was her minister, who agreed to do their counseling *after* the ceremony, since the couple seemed to be so well suited and ready for marriage.

"We just don't understand why you are rushing things," Sandy probed when she and Pete sat down with the couple.

"Why can't you be more supportive?" Brian countered. "Kendra's parents think it's admirable that we want to get married when so many couples are deciding to just live together these days."

Sandy had a host of reasons she and Pete were not on board—starting with the fact that it was a "rebound" relationship between two stubborn, immature people—but Brian had made up his mind, and at age thirty-one, he clearly felt he no longer needed to take counsel from his parents.

"Brian is an adult," Pete conceded as he and Sandy discussed their son's plans. "And our role has changed. We used to protect and provide for our kids. But now it's a balancing act. We can offer them the wisdom of our experience, but we can't interfere. All we can do is pray—and trust God."

Sandy knew her husband was right. But when Brian and Kendra decided to bump up their wedding date, shaving five months off the yearlong engagement, she struggled to keep the fear from rising up in her throat. Even Abby, the big sister who took her brother's side on virtually every issue, sensed that something was amiss. She desperately wanted to support her brother, but she could not pretend to be happy about his decision.

As the wedding date drew near, Sandy continued to ask God to stop what looked like a hasty and ill-considered union. But God stayed silent, and Sandy began to wonder whether she ought to hold her tongue too. She remembered what happened to Miriam when she spoke out against her brother Moses for marrying a foreigner: God got angry and struck her with leprosy![5] Sandy wasn't really worried that she'd get some awful disease, but she was wise enough to know that if God was at work, she should not get in the way.

Still, though, it was hard to control her emotions. And when the wedding day arrived and she found Abby weeping in her bedroom, it got even harder.

"So how did you get through that?" I asked, when Sandy described the situation to me. (Having recently married off two of my own daughters to young men we love, I could not begin to imagine how difficult it would be to watch my son get married to someone I had reservations about—and if I had found one of his sisters in a puddle of tears on his wedding day, that might have undone me!)

"I told Abby she had to get up because we were all in this together. We could be hateful and bitter, or we could choose to love Kendra and welcome her into our family."

"When did that happen?" I pressed. "When did you decide to stop asking God to prevent the wedding and start asking him to bless the couple?"

"When they walked down the aisle."

"Seriously?"

---

5. Numbers 12:1–15.

"Yes, seriously. The engagement chapter was closed, and a new chapter had begun. Two of the verses I had been praying over Brian spoke to my heart. Proverbs 18:22 says that he who finds a wife finds what is good and receives favor from the Lord. And James 1:17 says that every good and perfect gift is from the Lord. I realized that my son had found a wife, and that instead of criticizing her, I needed to see her as God's good and perfect gift for him, and be thankful."

Prayer Principle

Praising God changes our perspective and releases supernatural peace, hope, and joy.

Sandy's decision to choose trust and gratitude over things like bitterness and confusion reminded me of something Merlin Carothers wrote in his book *Power in Praise*: "To praise God is to express our acceptance of something that God is permitting to happen . . . When we sincerely accept and thank God for a situation, believing that He has allowed it to come about, there is released into that situation a supernatural, divine force that causes changes beyond what can be explained as an unfolding of natural events."[6]

Sure enough, as the months went by, *genuine* joy followed

---

6. Merlin Carothers, *Power in Praise: How the Spiritual Dynamic of Praise Revolutionizes Lives* (Escondido, CA: Carothers, 1972), 2, 13.

chosen joy in Sandy's heart. Kendra's strong will and stubborn spirit proved to be an asset as she stepped into her role as wife to an older man, matching her wits to his. And the fact that she came from such a large family turned out to be a huge plus, as Kendra was always quick to pitch in with kitchen cleanup and other chores when the families got together. Clearly, she knew what it took to keep a busy household running smoothly; she would, Sandy had to admit, make a wonderful mother.

Sandy has grown to love and admire her daughter-in-law. But she would be the first to tell you that the whole "meshing" thing has not come easily. She and Kendra have butted heads more than once, and Sandy has had to repeatedly remind herself to give God time to work—on both of them. And even more importantly, she and Pete have had to ask Brian and Kendra to forgive them for their harsh words and for the times when they allowed their uncertainty to triumph over their trust.

"It is a healing process," Sandy concedes. "But Brian and Kendra know we love them, and we know they love us—and with God's grace, we are all moving on, trusting God to knit our hearts together according to his design."

Poised for Prayer

More than a few moms and dads I spoke with are praying for adult children who are still single, either because (like Mariah and Henry, the couple you met in chapter 3) they've chosen living together over marriage or because they haven't yet found the "right" one.

Some of these parents have taken the "persistent widow" approach Jesus outlined in Luke 18 as an example of how we should "always pray and not give up."[7] Others have amended their request, asking God to fill their children with joy and a sense of purpose as they embrace singleness in the way Paul did—as a very real gift from God.[8] In all cases—in the parents who are asking God to give their children a spouse, in those who are praying for joy in the single life, and in those who are praying *both* prayers—the richest, most powerful prayers I heard were those that focused on an adult child's identity.

=====   *Prayer Principle*   =====

Pray that your child's sense of identity and worth will be found in Christ rather than in being single or married.

"I don't want my daughter to be defined by her marital status," one mother said. "The secret to happiness and security can't be found in a relationship with another person; it can only be found in Christ. And so I pray that my daughter will not feel pressured to get married or think that doing so will be what

---

7. Luke 18:1.
8. 1 Corinthians 7:7.

brings completeness to her life. I pray that she will know she is God's beloved—and that he is hers."

What a wise mama! I love her prayer, which is an excerpt from the Bible's most beautiful love song.[9] I am praying it for my married children and for those who are still single. And I am praying it for myself. Because in a life that is sometimes marked by disappointment, longing, and uncertainty, this song shines the spotlight on the most important things: the knowledge that our security is in Christ, and the certainty that we are his beloved.

---

9. See Song of Songs 6:3.

Prayers You Can Use

For Yourself

Heavenly Father . . .

When I find it hard to trust you, work in me to will and to act according to your good purpose. Help me to accept the things I don't like without complaining or arguing.
                                                PHILIPPIANS 2:13–14

As I pray for _____'s marital status, give me the oil of gladness instead of mourning, and a garment of praise instead of despair.   ISAIAH 61:3

Help me to teach and model goodness so that I can encourage _____ (daughter or daughter-in-law) to love her husband and children and be self-controlled, pure, and kind.   TITUS 2:3–5

For Your Children

Heavenly Father . . .

Whether _____ is married or single, help him recognize that his status is a gift from you.   1 CORINTHIANS 7:7

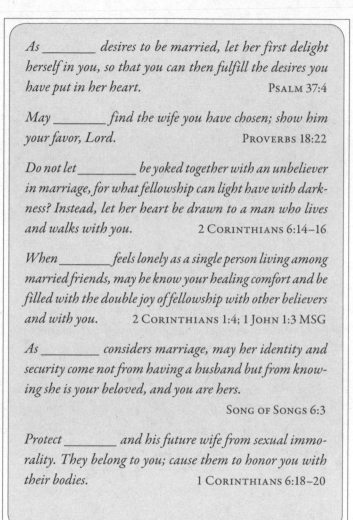

As _____ desires to be married, let her first delight herself in you, so that you can then fulfill the desires you have put in her heart. PSALM 37:4

May _____ find the wife you have chosen; show him your favor, Lord. PROVERBS 18:22

Do not let _____ be yoked together with an unbeliever in marriage, for what fellowship can light have with darkness? Instead, let her heart be drawn to a man who lives and walks with you. 2 CORINTHIANS 6:14–16

When _____ feels lonely as a single person living among married friends, may he know your healing comfort and be filled with the double joy of fellowship with other believers and with you. 2 CORINTHIANS 1:4; 1 JOHN 1:3 MSG

As _____ considers marriage, may her identity and security come not from having a husband but from knowing she is your beloved, and you are hers.

SONG OF SONGS 6:3

Protect _____ and his future wife from sexual immorality. They belong to you; cause them to honor you with their bodies. 1 CORINTHIANS 6:18–20

May _____ choose a wife who is worthy of respect, not a malicious talker, and trustworthy in everything.

1 TIMOTHY 3:11

May _____ choose a husband who will treat her with honor, recognizing her as an equal partner in your gift of new life. 1 PETER 3:7 NLT

Let _____ enjoy a marriage marked by mutual love, submission, self-sacrifice, caring, unity, and respect.

EPHESIANS 5:24–32

Every good and perfect gift is from you, Lord. Send _____ the gift of a spouse. JAMES 1:17

Shape _____ into a woman whose husband can have full confidence in her. Let her bring him good, not harm. Give her vigor and generosity. Clothe her with strength and dignity. May she speak with wisdom and faithful instruction. Equip _____ to watch over the affairs of her household, and may her husband praise her. Let her realize that charm is deceptive and beauty is fleeting, but a woman who fears the Lord is to be praised.

FROM PROVERBS 31, A PRAYER FOR A
DAUGHTER OR DAUGHTER-IN-LAW

Make _____ into a man who fears you and finds great delight in your commands. Should you grant him children, may they be upright and blessed. Give him wealth and riches, along with a righteousness that endures. Let him be generous and conduct his affairs with justice. May he be a man who has no fear of bad news; give him a steadfast heart and equip him to trust you. Bring him honor.

FROM PSALM 112, A PRAYER
FOR A SON OR SON-IN-LAW

CHAPTER 7

Praying for a Young Marriage

"A man will leave his father and mother and be united to his wife, and the two will become one flesh." This is a profound mystery.

EPHESIANS 5:31–32

"Marriage is glorious but hard. It's a burning joy and strength, and yet it is also blood, sweat, and tears, humbling defeats and exhausting victories. No marriage I know more than a few weeks old could be described as a fairy tale come true."[1]

That's how Timothy Keller begins the first chapter in his book *The Meaning of Marriage*. I think it's a great book, and I love to give it to newly engaged couples, but I always do so a bit apologetically, like I know they might rather have something from Pottery Barn. "Don't be discouraged by all that stuff Keller

---

1. Timothy Keller, *The Meaning of Marriage: Facing the Complexities of Commitment with the Wisdom of God* (New York: Dutton, 2011), 13.

writes about marriage being painful," I say, trying to grease the skids a bit. "It can be sometimes—but it's definitely worth it!"

One of the most "glorious but hard" hurdles that must be scaled early on is the whole idea of "leaving and cleaving"— which is how the King James Version describes what happens in marriage.[2] As Keller puts it, God didn't put a parent and a child in the garden; he put a husband and wife. "God asks that a man leave his father and mother, as powerful as that relationship may have been, to forge a new union that must be an even more important and powerful force in his life."[3]

For some couples, that's an easy transition; for others, it's excruciating. Robbie and I used to teach a marriage class at our church, and we heard any number of stories. The bride who, having moved across the country because of her new husband's job, cried every single day for three months—and called her mother every night. The groom who would stop at his parents' home for a drink after work—leaving his wife of two years alone at home, trying to make dinner, tidy the house, and bathe their one-year-old son before bedtime. The wife whose marriage of twelve years was crumbling under the strain of a domineering mother-in-law—and a husband who always took his mom's side.

Most of the material Robbie and I used in our class came from The Marriage Course, designed by the folks at Alpha

---

2. Genesis 2:24 KJV.
3. Ibid., 139.

International.[4] In one session, they say that even couples who have been married for many years may need to ask themselves whether they have "fully left" their parents. "Is one of our parents more important to us than our partner? Are we still emotionally dependent on our parents? Are they trying to control our lives? Do we expect our marriage to look like their marriage?"[5]

That last question—about what we expect our marriage to look like—was something that nearly derailed my own marriage early on. I grew up in a home where my father was a big help in the kitchen. Mom did most of the cooking, but Dad was the one who went to the grocery store (something he did almost every day on the way home from work), and after dinner, he'd commandeer the kitchen for the cleanup duty. We kids helped, but Dad had spent time in the Navy, and he was clearly the one at the helm.

Robbie had pretty much the opposite experience. I am not sure his father knew where the grocery store was. His mother did all things domestic—the shopping, the cooking, the cleaning, the putting away. She was genuinely happy in this role (and she still is; if you offer to help, she just shoos you away). And so Robbie's dad would come home at night, open a beer, and read the newspaper. He sat in the kitchen throughout their nightly

---

4. Alpha International, "The Marriage Courses," https://alphausa.org/the-marriage-courses (accessed April 11, 2017).
5. Nicky and Sila Lee, *The Marriage Book: How to Build a Lasting Relationship* (Deerfield, IL: Alpha, 2000), 207.

routine—which, I guess, in his mind was showing support for his wife while she worked.

When Robbie and I returned from our honeymoon to begin our wedded bliss, you can imagine what happened. We'd get home from work and stare at each other. I'd wonder where the groceries were; he'd sit there with his drink and his paper and wonder where the meal was. Wanting to be a good wife, I quickly adapted. I resolved to be just like his mother. I didn't cook half as well as she did, but I figured I could at least try.

Robbie and I went on like that—me shopping and cooking and cleaning, him drinking and reading and watching—for more than a year. But I was getting tired (and a little bit grumpy), so I started dropping hints to indicate that I'd welcome some help. But Robbie didn't seem to get them. So I started nagging. And sometimes that worked—Robbie would pour the water or whatever—but he would never do it quite the way my father had.

He was doomed. We both were.

I wanted to complain to my mother, but I knew she wouldn't listen. "If you and Robbie ever have a fight," she had told me back before we were married, "you are not welcome to come home." She said it with a smile, but I knew what she meant: She wanted me to be on Robbie's team, for better or for worse, and she wasn't going to do anything that might help create distance between us.

Not knowing what else to do, I decided to take my case up with God. "Robbie doesn't help out like my dad did," I said. "I don't mind being the main cook, but I am just as tired as he is when I get home from work, and I wish I didn't have to ask him to pitch in every night."

"Jodie," I sensed God say, "it's going to be okay. If you will stop nagging Robbie and start trusting me, I will make him into a better husband than anything you could have asked for or imagined. Even if I gave you free rein to create what you think of as the perfect man, it wouldn't come close to what I have in mind."

Okay then. I agreed to back off. And that very night (it was more than thirty years ago, but I still remember chopping broccoli in our tiny newlywed kitchen), Robbie came around the corner from the tiny newlywed living room. "Can I do anything to help with dinner?" he asked.

I burst into tears. In more than a year of marriage, he had never once asked that question. Poor Robbie was at a loss. He had no idea what to do; he'd offered to help, and now his young bride was crying. I am sure most newlywed husbands (and plenty of oldyweds too) have found themselves in the same spot, unable to read their wife's mind and at a loss as to how to explain her tears. In my case, I was just so incredibly grateful—to Robbie and to God.

I wish I could say I stopped nagging forever (I didn't), but I learned a lesson that day, one I've tried to teach my own children: We can't change anybody. That's what God does. He's the one who invented leaving and cleaving. He's the one who says he will work in us to "will and to act" according to his good purpose.[6]

---

6. Philippians 2:13.

And he's the one who has promised to finish the good work that he starts in our lives.[7]

===================== *Prayer Principle* =====================

We do the praying; God does the changing.

Thirty years later, Robbie and I had to learn the art of leaving and cleaving all over again—this time as parents. Our two oldest daughters, Hillary and Annesley, got married within four months of each other, at the very same altar where Robbie and I said our vows. At the rehearsal, the minister asked whether Robbie planned to say "I do" or "her mother and I do" in answer to the "Who gives this woman?" question. Robbie chose the longer version—but told me (both times) that he was worried he wouldn't be able to get all five words out without a catch in his voice. I knew what he meant. We were thrilled for our girls—and we adored their guys—but in giving them up, in letting them go, we knew we'd be doing more than just closing a chapter; we'd be finishing a whole book (one we had savored) so that a brand-new story could begin.

I had prayed for these husbands since before our girls were born; as soon as I learned I was pregnant, I began asking God to bless and care for my child's eventual spouse and to bring

---

7. Philippians 1:6.

him (or her) into our lives in his perfect timing. And now here they were: Geoff and Charlie—two living, breathing, handsome answers to prayer! The only blemish I could find on either young man was the fact that he had graduated from Virginia Tech. They *both* had.

(Which, for a U.Va. fan, is tough. Especially during football season.)

Anyhow, I had prayed for my girls, and I had prayed for these boys, for twenty-five years. And now my prayers were going to have to change. I would still pray for *her*, and I'd still pray for *him*, but there was a whole lot of *them* that I'd need to start covering. And remembering the early days of my own marriage, I knew I'd need to pray about their different backgrounds and ask God to give them patience and understanding as they learned to let go of their own families and traditions and hold fast to one another.

═══════════ *Prayer Principle* ═══════════

When your children get married, your prayers take on a new dimension. Now you're not just praying for him or for her; you're also praying for *them*.

I found a wealth of helpful prayer prompts in the Bible as I read about real people and the way they adjusted to married life. For instance, I didn't like to think of Ruth leaving her family behind, but I loved the way she honored her widowed mother-in-law, saying, "Where you go I will go, and where you stay I will stay. Your people will be my people and your God my God."[8] I asked God to create that same sense of connection between Annesley and Hillary and their new mothers-in-law, one that would quickly let them all know that they had become each other's "people."

And I loved the way Moses related to his father-in-law, Jethro. The two men clearly had a strong bond, and Jethro was thrilled to hear how God had rescued the Israelites and sustained them during their desert hardships. But when he saw all the people crowding around Moses, telling him their problems, he realized his son-in-law was getting worn-out. "The work is too heavy for you," he said. "You cannot handle it alone. Listen now to me and I will give you some advice."[9]

Moses took Jethro's counsel (which essentially involved teaching the people God's laws and appointing judges to settle their cases), and everyone was satisfied. I didn't know if or when Geoff or Charlie would need to confide in Robbie, but I figured the time would come, so I asked God to give them a Moses-and-Jethro relationship, one where the guys felt free to talk about the good things God had done in their careers or their marriages, but also to be honest about any challenges they might face and know they could come to Robbie for advice or direction about what they should do.

8. Ruth 1:16.
9. Exodus 18:18–19.

=== *Prayer Principle* ===

Consider using the example of biblical characters—real
people, with real relationships and real problems—
to shape your prayers for your children.[10]

In addition to these in-law prayers, I cultivated a whole bunch
of general prayers over both couples in their newlywed lives,
prayers like the ones listed at the end of this chapter. I covered
everything I could think of, from where they would live to how
they would treat each other to the way they'd grow in their love
for each other and for God.

But then, before I had even taken the girls' wedding dresses
to the cleaners and while the UPS man was still pulling up to the
house with things like slow cookers and cutlery, the differences in
background and perspectives began to make themselves known.

From an organizational standpoint, Robbie and I had always
considered Annesley our best work. She's the one who, if you
recall from *Praying the Scriptures for Your Children*, used to lay
her clothes out before school every night—and then make a list
of what she planned to wear and put it on top of the pile, just
to be safe. Her bed was always made and her notebooks clean
and tidy, and when we traveled, she kept our passports in her
backpack, since we knew we could count on her not to lose them.

---

10. For examples of and information about using biblical characters to shape
your prayers, see the appendix in *Praying the Scriptures for Your Children*.

I was sure Annesley would have Geoff straightened out in no time. (I had no evidence he needed straightening, other than the fact that he was a boy.) What I didn't know—what I couldn't have known—was that Geoff's idea of "organized" made Annesley's housekeeping style look like she'd left in a hurry, like maybe she was wanted by the FBI. Geoff grew up in a home where (as his mother will tell you), everything was "table, table, lamp, lamp"—all perfectly matched and efficient. Annesley grew up in a home that I like to think of as tidy . . . but if you come over for dinner, please don't open any closets. Or drawers.

It wasn't long before Annesley, awash in a sea of wedding boxes and tissue (and with nowhere near enough cabinet space to store all their new platters), began to lose heart. Throw in regular visits from the beloved dog she shared with her former roommate—one who left piles of hair (and sometimes worse) in his wake—and we both began to worry that Geoff's patience might wear thin. Not knowing what else to do, I gave him a lint brush for Easter and started praying verses like Ephesians 4:2 over their marriage: "May Geoff and Annesley be completely humble, gentle, and patient; may they bear with one another in love."

Meanwhile, Charlie was looking at Hillary, wide-eyed. He'd spent most of his life as an only child in a home where thoughts were processed before spoken and silence held as much value as conversation. When he and Hillary sat down to dinner—or worse, when he came to family dinners at our house, where four

Berndt women all had stories to tell—he took on the look of one who'd been blitzkrieged. "You people never stop talking," he finally said, about five months into their marriage. "You always interrupt each other. And you always think you are right. I wanted to ask a question about something that somebody said a few minutes ago, but now I don't even know what it was."

We all stared at Charlie, guilty as charged. "Charlie," I said, as gently as possible, "you gotta learn to keep up."

I was kidding (sort of), but Charlie's comment gave me a window into the very different communication styles that he and Hillary had grown up with, and it showed me a fresh way to pray. "May Hillary be quick to listen and slow to speak," I asked, drawing on the wisdom of James 1:19. And knowing that my daughter was a natural-born talker (as are all the Berndt women), I added the verse that got our family through about a hundred endless car trips: "Let no unwholesome talk come out of Hillary's mouth, but only what is helpful for building Charlie up, that her words would benefit him."[11]

I don't know how your family has been formed or what your child's particular leaving-and-cleaving challenges will be. I do know, however, that even the most well-suited couples, from the most similar backgrounds, will find themselves tested. Because you may think you know the person you are marrying (or the person your child is marrying), but you don't. As Timothy Keller

---

11. Ephesians 4:29.

puts it, "Marriage brings you into more intense proximity to another human being than any other relationship can. Therefore, the moment you marry someone, you and your spouse begin to change in profound ways, and you can't know ahead of time what these changes will be. So you don't know, you can't know, who your spouse will actually be in the future until you get there."[12]

Poised for Prayer

In some ways, leaving and cleaving are two sides of the same coin. Marriage is, ideally, the closest relationship two people will ever know. Some might argue that the parent-child bond takes this honor (because, after all, a child's life actually begins within his mother), but authors Nicky and Sila Lee draw an important distinction. "A healthy parent-child relationship is to be one of increasing separation and growing *independence*," they write, but marriage is a relationship where two people, "at one time strangers to each other . . . enter into a relationship marked, at its best, by increasing *interdependence*."[13]

It is this growing interdependence that we are privileged to endorse—and to pray for—on behalf of our children. I am sure there are countless links in the chain, but I'll share just four prayer areas that can help forge a strong union:

---

12. Keller, *The Meaning of Marriage*, 33.
13. Lee, *The Marriage Book*, 17.

1. *Make it not "all about me."* In an age where marriage is
   often seen as a means to happiness and personal fulfillment, it can be easy to adopt a self-centered attitude. I'm
   asking God to flip that upside down for my kids, marking
   their marriages with the Christlike beauty of Philippians
   2:3–4: "In humility value others above yourselves, not
   looking to your own interests but each of you to the
   interests of the others."

2. *Let them be each other's best friend.* I love romance (who
   doesn't?), but even the most passionate relationship
   cannot satisfy where friendship is lacking. I pray that
   my children and their spouses will be the kind of friend
   who "loves at all times" and that they will sharpen one
   another "as iron sharpens iron," making each other wiser,
   better, and stronger.[14]

3. *May they be quick to forgive.* Marriage, more than any
   other relationship, reveals hidden character traits (and
   sometimes flaws). As I pray for my children and their
   spouses, I'm asking God to fill their relationship with the
   1 Corinthians 13 kind of love, the kind that is patient,
   kind, and keeps no record of wrongs. I'm asking that they
   would learn to resolve their differences, not going to bed
   angry (and giving bitterness a chance to grow).[15] More

---

14. Proverbs 17:17; 27:17.
15. Ephesians 4:26–27.

than anything, I want them to "bear with each other and forgive one another," just as God forgave them.[16]

4. *May their love and their lives be filled with the Holy Spirit.* Ephesians 5:21 offers a great recipe for marital success: "Submit to one another out of reverence for Christ." The trouble is, we can't really do this—we can't even come close—without the Holy Spirit's help. So I'm backing up and starting with verse 18, where Paul writes, "Be filled with the Spirit." When that happens—when we start with an infilling of God's Spirit—it informs how we speak to one another, how we worship, and how able we are to give thanks.[17] With a Spirit-filled marriage, all good things are possible.

---

16. Colossians 3:13.
17. Ephesians 5:19–20.

Prayers You Can Use

For Yourself

Heavenly Father...

You liken children to "arrows in the hands of a warrior." Help me remember that arrows are designed to fly, and when I feel the sting of release, let me be grateful for all that you have done and for all that you have in store.

PSALM 127:4

May I parent _____ with an eye toward training her not to be dependent on me, but to love and care for her husband and children.   TITUS 2:4

Help me take delight in your commands (including the one about leaving and cleaving); thank you for blessing my children.   PSALM 112:1–2

For Your Children

The following prayers are excerpted from "The Celebration and Blessing of a Marriage" in the *Book of Common Prayer*. Robbie and I prayed these words over

Hillary and Charlie and Annesley and Geoff during their wedding ceremonies, and we continue to pray these same blessings for them today. The references that accompany each prayer represent my own thoughts about where these promises may be drawn out of Scripture; I'm sure the original writers had a biblical literacy that far exceeds my own and may have had additional or different verses in mind when they crafted these beautiful prayers.

Heavenly Father . . .

Look with favor upon the world you have made, and for which your Son gave his life, and especially upon _____ *and* _____, *whom you make one flesh in Holy Matrimony.*

LEVITICUS 26:9; JOHN 3:16; MARK 10:8

Give _____ *and* _____ *wisdom and devotion in the ordering of their common life, that each may be to the other a strength in need, a counselor in perplexity, a comfort in sorrow, and a companion in joy.*

PROVERBS 27:17; PROVERBS 27:9;
2 CORINTHIANS 1:4; ECCLESIASTES 4:9–10;
PSALM 149:5

Grant that their wills may be so knit together in your will, and their spirits in your Spirit, that _____ and _____ may grow in love and peace with you and one another all the days of their life.   PSALM 40:8; GALATIANS 5:25; 2 CORINTHIANS 13:11; PSALM 23:6

Give _____ and _____ grace, when they hurt each other, to recognize and acknowledge their fault and to seek each other's forgiveness and yours.

2 CORINTHIANS 13:14; EPHESIANS 2:8; HEBREWS 12:15; COLOSSIANS 3:13

Make _____ and _____'s life together a sign of Christ's love to this sinful and broken world, that unity may overcome estrangement, forgiveness may heal guilt, and joy may conquer despair.   JOHN 13:34–35; ROMANS 5:8; JOHN 17:23; ROMANS 8:1; ISAIAH 61:3

Bestow on _____ and _____, if it is your will, the gift and heritage of children and the grace to bring them up to know you, to love you, and to serve you.

PSALM 127:3; PROVERBS 22:6

Give _____ and _____ such fulfillment of their mutual affection that they may reach out in love and concern for others.

2 CORINTHIANS 9:11–13; 1 THESSALONIANS 3:12

CHAPTER 8

Praying through a Troubled Marriage or a Divorce

Be patient, bearing with one another in love.
EPHESIANS 4:2

"Don't marry someone who is not a Christian."

That's a piece of advice that most parents I interviewed for this book have given their children, and it's one that my friend Betsy sees as critical for building a strong and lasting union. Every relationship is bound to have its rocky moments, but, as Betsy told me, "At least if you have a partner in Christ, you will have that common bond, and you can fight your battles together."

At least that's how Betsy thought things were supposed to work. And when Betsy and Tom's daughter called to say she might have found "the one," they were thrilled.

"I told him I was a Christian on our first date," Casey gushed, "and that that was really important to me. And guess what? He said that was great, because he is too!"

An accomplished athlete, Jackson had played soccer in

college, which was where he'd given his life to the Lord. Now, six years later, he had channeled his competitive drive into his sales job with a software company, and it showed. As handsome as he was successful, he and Casey made a striking pair as they attended church together each Sunday. And when Jackson popped the question, everyone (including Matthew, the young couple's minister) thought it was a match made in heaven. Two passionate and energetic people, Jackson and Casey were sure to set the world on fire.

It wasn't long before Casey began to feel the heat.

Several months into their marriage, Jackson didn't seem as thoughtful or kind as he had before. Sometimes his comments made her feel incompetent, as though she had failed at some aspect of married life. Was that normal? Was she being too sensitive? She didn't know.

"Oh, honey," Betsy said when Casey confided her concerns, "you just want everything to be perfect. But every newlywed couple goes through an adjustment period. It's going to be okay—you just have to remember not to be selfish. Marriage is all about sharing and putting each other first."

Surely that's all it was—two self-centered young people learning to live with each other. Betsy wasn't worried. And then, as if proving that things were all right, Casey called with the news that she was pregnant.

When the baby arrived (a boy), the proud grandparents took any opportunity they could to make the three-hour drive to visit the young family. Casey was still working part-time, and she and Jackson welcomed the extra help.

"Seriously, Mom," Casey said, during one of their visits, "thank you for coming. Sometimes I feel like such an idiot. Like, Jackson will come home from work and ask me why I couldn't get the dishes done. Or he'll get mad if something isn't the way he thinks it should be, and he'll say things like, 'How can you call yourself a good mom?'"

Betsy wanted to believe that Casey was just being dramatic, that Jackson couldn't be that cruel or insensitive, but she and Tom had seen enough to know there was an ugly side to their son-in-law. He made no effort to help out around the house, and yet he didn't try to hide his disdain for what he saw as Casey's domestic shortcomings. Considering some of the terse or derisive comments he made in front of his in-laws, Betsy could only imagine the things he said when she and Tom were not around.

"Maybe this is just the way Jackson thinks husbands talk to their wives," she confided to Tom when they were alone together. "Maybe it's how his dad treated his mother, like it's a pattern or something."

"Could be," Tom agreed. "Let's pray to break any generational bonds or patterns of evil."

Together, Betsy and Tom read verses like Ezekiel 18:20 — "The child will not share the guilt of the parent" — and asked God to step in and break any bad habits that Jackson might have learned as a child. They also prayed for Casey's physical and emotional protection and borrowed a line from the Lord's Prayer, asking that the couple would be "delivered from evil."[1] Knowing how negative communication patterns can sometimes hold people captive, they clung to verses like Luke 4:18, where Jesus says he was sent "to proclaim freedom for prisoners."

=== *Prayer Principle* ===

Destructive family patterns can be broken. Ask God
to break these bonds and set your children free.

For a time, it looked as though their prayers had been answered. Casey got pregnant again, and the young family seemed to be thriving. But the next time Betsy and Tom visited, they could tell things were not okay. Casey, normally so lighthearted and confident, seemed uncertain and withdrawn.

"I know Jackson loves me," she said, when Betsy pressed for details. "He always sends me flowers or writes some sort of sweet card to apologize after he criticizes me or gets angry, so I know he knows what he is doing is wrong. But . . ."

A tear slid down Casey's cheek, and Betsy saw Tom's jaw clench.

"I am going to speak to him," he said.

"No, Dad!" Casey protested. "Please don't do that. I don't

---

1. Matthew 6:13.

know how he would take it. I know you mean well, but it could backfire."

"But Casey," Tom countered, "I can't just sit by and watch him hurt you. No father could do that! What if it gets physical?"

"Please, Dad," Casey implored, her voice soft. "I'm not in any danger. I would know if it came to that. I am just really sad. Will you and Mom please just pray?"

Tom agreed to keep praying, but he and Betsy also met privately with Matthew, the minister, and described the patterns they had seen in the marriage, patterns that seemed to mirror relationships marked by alcoholism, infidelity, or physical abuse.

"We know Jackson loves Casey, but sometimes . . ." Tom glanced at Betsy, as if to apologize for what he was about to say. "Sometimes I just want to beat him up!"

Matthew shook his head. "I am so sorry," he said. "I knew Casey was sad, but I thought she just missed being away from you all. We will help."

True to his word, the minister and others from the church came alongside the young couple. An older woman began meeting regularly with Casey, offering her communication strategies to use in the face of Jackson's cutting words and helping her formulate a plan for what she could do if she and the children ever felt like they were in physical danger. Meanwhile, Matthew arranged for Jackson to be mentored by a businessman he respected. Little by little, things began to improve. When their second grandchild (a girl) was born several months later,

Betsy and Tom breathed a sigh of relief. Maybe they had finally turned a corner.

But then Betsy's phone rang. It was Casey, and she was crying.

"Jackson didn't come home last night," she said. "I was worried sick, but then he showed up this morning with an apology note."

"Oh, honey," Betsy said, sinking into a chair, "what did you do?"

"I pulled out a stack of letters just like it, Mom! I've kept them all. I looked at him and said, 'You've written these notes to me *over* and *over* again. You buy me presents. You *always* say you're sorry for whatever you said or whatever you did. So how am I supposed to believe you now?'"

Betsy was quiet for a moment. "What did he say to that?" she finally asked.

"He said he loves me. And I know he does. And I love him—truly. But . . ." Casey's voice faltered.

"But what?"

"But he's checking my phone now. And my email. So Mom, please don't text me, okay?"

Betsy felt her heart skip a beat. "Oh, Casey," she said, "I know you love Jackson. But you can't continue to live this way, under these destructive patterns. You have those babies to think about."

"I know," Casey sniffed. "Can Daddy get me a lawyer?"

What God hath joined together let no one put asunder.

The words from the marriage ceremony came, unbidden,

to Betsy's mind. She and Tom had spent most of Casey's life rescuing her from anything they perceived to be dangerous or too difficult. More than anything, she wanted to step in again now, to pull her daughter out of what was clearly an awful situation. It seemed, however, that God was asking them to stand down.

Betsy wasn't sure she had the courage to step aside, but she knew she had to try—and she felt sure Tom would agree. They couldn't become agents of separation, not unless the situation became truly unsafe for Casey or the grandchildren.

"Casey," she said slowly, "you can call a lawyer if you want to, but Daddy and I can't do that. Not yet. But we'll figure something out. God will provide."

Betsy sounded a lot calmer than she felt. How long was a woman supposed to endure such a gut-wrenching tide of emotional abuse? The scars were already vivid; anyone who knew Casey could see them. Casey had lost her confidence, as well as her joy.

Later that night, she filled Tom in on how the situation seemed to be deteriorating. "It's not good," Betsy said. "And I hate to admit it, but I'm not sure I see any fix."

"I know," Tom said, struggling to keep his voice steady. "And it makes me crazy. But . . ."

"But what?"

"Jackson is not the enemy."

Betsy closed her eyes. She knew what Tom meant. Casey's fight—their fight—wasn't with their son-in-law; it was against a much darker force. The words of Ephesians 6:12 flooded her mind: "Our struggle is not against flesh and blood, but against the rulers, against the authorities, against the powers of this dark world and against the spiritual forces of evil in the heavenly realms."

It was true that Jackson could be a jerk, and he had certainly hurt their daughter. At the end of the day, though, he wasn't the real enemy. The real enemy, Betsy knew, was Satan. He wanted to steal their joy, kill their hope, and destroy their marriage.

===== *Prayer Principle* =====

When you pray for your child's troubled marriage, remember that his or her spouse is not the enemy.

Armed with a fresh perspective as to who the "bad guy" was, Betsy and Tom tweaked their prayer strategy. They continued to pray for Casey, that God would keep her safe, help her overcome her fears, and show her how to trust.[2] They prayed that her identity would be grounded in Christ and that she would know, once again, that she was holy and dearly loved.[3] They prayed for forgiveness and healing.[4] But they added a new dimension to their petitions.

---

2. Isaiah 12:2.
3. Colossians 3:12.
4. 2 Chronicles 7:14.

Instead of getting angry with Jackson, they began to ask God to bless him and fill him with love, insight, and discernment.[5] They prayed for speech patterns to change, so that his words would encourage Casey and build her up.[6] And recognizing how much had been taken from the young family during the years of conflict, they borrowed a line from the prophet Joel, asking God to "repay them for the years the locusts had eaten."[7]

Fully aware there were unseen forces at work, they prayed that God would put a hedge of protection around the couple's marriage. They asked God to cover Casey and Jackson with spiritual armor—things like the shield of faith and the belt of truth—so that they could stand their ground against any attacks that might come their way.[8]

As they prayed, Betsy and Tom slowly sensed a shift. No longer did Casey telephone with cries for help; instead, her calls were punctuated with stories of a newfound peace and confidence as she learned to use communication techniques gleaned from the counselor at church and to rely on God's strength when she felt like she'd reached the end of her own. Casey's joy was gradually being restored.

For his part, Jackson continued to meet with his mentor and his words continued to soften. Watching him play soccer with his

---

5. Philippians 1:9–10.
6. Ephesians 4:29.
7. Joel 2:25.
8. Job 1:10; Ephesians 6:10–16.

son in the front yard, Betsy found it hard to believe he was the same man who would lash out at, or disappear from, his family.

=============== *Prayer Principle* ===============

When your children go through painful trials,
ask God to use their suffering to produce
perseverance, character, and hope.[9]

As difficult as it had been for them to "let go and let God," Betsy realized she and Tom were seeing the fulfillment of James 1:2–4 in their daughter's marriage. The trials Casey faced were being used by God to make her "mature and complete, not lacking anything." Six years into her marriage, she had a sense of identity and purpose that had nothing to do with her parents' faith and everything to do with her own. And in a twist that Betsy never could have predicted, Casey was using the wisdom she'd gained to help other young brides navigate their own marital struggles.

"I know Casey and Jackson's story isn't over," Betsy says. "There are still wounds that need healing, and there is still trust to rebuild. But God has done good things.

"This is probably an overused expression, but I believe God did a miracle."

---

9. Romans 5:3–4.

Poised for Prayer

"When you get married," Timothy Keller writes, "your spouse is a big truck driving right through your heart. Marriage brings out the worst in you. It doesn't create your weaknesses . . . it reveals them."[10]

Sometimes—as with Casey and Jackson—that revelation turns out to be a good thing, as couples learn where their individual flaws are and how to fix them. Sometimes, though, the hurt feels too great. Hard hearts, broken vows, repeated betrayals, and other wounds can leave one or both spouses bereft of any hope for healing.

I spoke with one father, Jim, who watched his son's marriage fall apart. David and Tara had gotten married, purchased a home, and had a daughter. They'd quit going to church and seemed to be drifting away from their faith, but Jim had no idea that the couple was also drifting away from one another—not until David called with the news that Tara wanted to move out and that she didn't love him anymore.

Jim and his wife, Joan, were devastated. "You pray for your children," he said, "and you would even die for them, but you cannot make their decisions for them. It gives you a glimpse into the heart of God and how he, as a Father, agonizes over us. That verse about how the Spirit prays for us with groans that words

---

10. Timothy Keller, *The Meaning of Marriage: Facing the Complexities of Commitment with the Wisdom of God* (New York: Dutton, 2011), 153.

cannot express makes more sense to me now than ever before. I know what it's like to pray that way."[11]

Was Jim, I wondered, angry with Tara for leaving his son?

"I don't know what happened between them," he said. "They are two very different people, and they live in a culture where most of their friends are divorced. It would be easy to try to blame someone—I could even blame myself, wondering what I could have done differently as a parent. But none of that really matters.

"I don't see Tara as a candidate for alienation," he continued. "I see her as a candidate for redemption. I don't want to say or do anything that could bring more division to our family; what I want is for David and Tara to know that they are loved."

I asked what that looked like, in practical terms.

Jim told me that, in addition to asking God to draw David and Tara back to faith (and even to each other), he prayed for himself, asking that God's love would just "ooze out" of him as a father, a father-in-law, and a grandfather. "We know that God is gracious and compassionate," he said, quoting Psalm 145, "and that he is slow to anger and rich in love. That's how I want to behave toward David and his family, even if he and Tara never reconcile. I don't know what the future holds, but I know God's promises are sure. 'Weeping may stay for the night, but rejoicing comes in the morning.'[12] That's what we are counting on."

If you have had to watch your child's marriage crumble over

---

11. Jim was referring to Romans 8:26.
12. Psalm 30:5.

hard-heartedness, infidelity, or some other pain, know that you are not alone. God knows what that feels like. He himself has been betrayed, and he has been through a divorce.[13] And yet he offers this powerful promise for us and for our children: "Israel, put your hope in the LORD, for with the LORD is unfailing love, and with him is full redemption."[14]

I don't want to ignore or minimize the immeasurable pain of a bad marriage or a divorce. But for believers—for those who put their hope in God—redemption is abundant, overflowing, and complete. Weeping may last through the night (and the night may be dark and long), but his promise is sure: joy really does come in the morning.[15]

---

13. Jeremiah 3:8.
14. Psalm 130:7.
15. Psalm 30:5 NLT.

Prayers You Can Use

For Yourself

Heavenly Father . . .

As I speak to and pray for _____ and _____, may the words of my mouth and the meditation of my heart be pleasing in your sight.   PSALM 19:14

When _____ causes grief to our family, help me to extend forgiveness, comfort, and love so that Satan might not outwit us.   2 CORINTHIANS 2:7–11

Out of the depths I cry to you, Lord. Hear my voice and let your ears be attentive to my cry for mercy.

PSALM 130:1–2

For Your Children

Heavenly Father . . .

May _____ and _____ be completely humble and gentle. May they be patient, bearing with one another in love.   EPHESIANS 4:2

Don't let _____ or _____ use foul or abusive language. Let everything they say be good and helpful, so that their words will be an encouragement to those who hear them.   Ephesians 4:29 NLT

Remind _____ and _____ that their struggle is not against one another, but against the spiritual forces of evil.   Ephesians 6:12

May _____ be quick to listen, slow to speak, and slow to become angry.   James 1:19

Put a hedge of protection around _____ and their household and everything they have.   Job 1:10

Help _____ and _____ to make allowance for each other's faults and forgive each other when they are offended.   Colossians 3:13

May _____ and _____ revere you. Be the sun of righteousness in their lives and bring healing to their relationship.   Malachi 4:2

Repay _____ for the years the locusts have eaten. May they know you are their God, and may they never again be ashamed.   Joel 2:25–27

May _____ give honor to his wife, _____, and treat her with understanding as they live together, so that his prayers will not be hindered.   1 PETER 3:7 NLT

Give _____ and _____ endurance and encouragement, as well as a spirit of unity, so that with one heart and one mouth they may glorify you, Lord.

ROMANS 15:5–6

Cause _____ to put his hope in you. Cover him with your unfailing love, and bless him with full redemption.

PSALM 130:7

When weeping stays for the night, show _____ your joy in the morning.   PSALM 30:5

PART 3

PRAYING
through the Milestones
in Your ADULT CHILD'S LIFE

CHAPTER 9

Praying for a Good Place to Live

God began by making one person, and
from him came all the different people who
live everywhere in the world. God decided
exactly when and where they must live.

Acts 17:26 NCV

Robbie and I were proud of Virginia when she landed a summer internship in New York City. We were not sure, though, where she would live. We didn't know a lot about the city, but we had heard that finding an affordable place to rent could be tough.

"Don't worry," Virginia said, with her characteristic optimism. "A lot of my friends are working in New York; I'm sure I can find a good sublease for a few months."

Maybe I would have been wise to remember my father-in-law's description of Virginia when she was about ten years old. "That girl," he said, "is seldom right, but never in doubt." But "that girl" had grown up okay, and when she said she could find someplace to live, we figured she could.

And she did.

We gave her some time to get settled, and then, a few weeks after she started her job, I went up for a visit. I gave Virginia's address to the taxi driver who had picked me up at the airport, but when he pulled up to her door after dark, I was sure he was mistaken. "This can't be it," I said, eyeing the neon lights of the strip club that seemed to take up most of the building.

"Oh, this is it," the driver said. "You are here."

And sure enough, Virginia popped out of a nearby doorway, all smiles. "Don't mind the smell," she said, grabbing my suitcase. "They park the carriages under our building at night—and I guess they keep the horses in there too. It's kind of a stable."

The good news, if I can stretch the modifier, was that the apartment was easy to clean (it held just three pieces of furniture: a sofa, a small table and two chairs, and a bed tucked behind a white curtain), and if you got very close to the window and craned your neck in just the right way, you could see the Hudson River—a water view!—behind what looked to be warehouses.

And to Virginia's credit, the place was affordable.

Needless to say, I was glad it was just for the summer . . . and that I knew some good prayer verses to use as I asked God to keep my girl safe!

Finding a good place to live is never easy, and for many

young adults, the process can be daunting. Factors like budget, neighborhood, condition of the dwelling, amenities, security, commute time to work, and roommates may all play a part in the decision; it can seem (and it often is) impossible to tick all the boxes on the wish list. As newlyweds, Hillary and Charlie were willing to give up things like a dishwasher and central air conditioning in order to live in an old-house-turned-duplex that was close to the ocean; as a young professional, Annesley opted to live with a gal she had never met because she figured that having a roommate—even one who was a total stranger—would be a good way to both defray costs and ward off loneliness.

A quick spin through my network of praying friends reveals any number of housing trade-offs and challenges. Some of my peers worry that their kids are not living in a "nice enough" neighborhood, while others fear that their children, eager to stake claim to a desirable lifestyle, will bite off more than they can afford to chew. And some of our young adults haven't moved out at all—or if they have, they've come back.

Most of these "home again" kids have moved back temporarily, generally for financial reasons, but there are other factors—like medical conditions and special needs—that can delay or complicate the transition to independence. Not only do these parents find themselves considering details like affordability and location; they must also weigh (and pray about) the quality of care their adult children will receive, if and when they leave home.

Amanda has four adult children, one of whom has Down Syndrome. "I often feel more protective of her than I do toward my other kids," she says, "but I pray a lot of the same prayers and rely on a lot of the same promises, like Psalm 121, where God says he will watch over our coming and our going. No matter where my daughter is or where she lives, I need to trust God to keep her from harm.

"And," she continues, "I ask God to give me strength. Anybody can soar like an eagle. But when you are going through a desert (and that's what it feels like when you have an adult child living at home and you're not sure how long that situation will last), you need the second part of that promise: that you will be able to walk—day in and day out—and not be faint."[1]

Prayer Principle

Finding a good place to live can take time.
Ask God to give your children (and you, if they are
at home) the strength to "walk and not be faint."

I remember what it felt like to need God's strength back when Robbie and I wanted to buy our first home. We only knew two things about real estate: it was important to buy in the right neighborhood ("location, location, location"), and we shouldn't

---

1. Isaiah 40:31.

spend more than 25 percent of our take-home pay on a fifteen-year mortgage.[2] Unfortunately, the first rule didn't square with the second. All the houses we liked—the cute ones in established neighborhoods that had things like good schools, parks, and lots of happy-looking children—seemed to be out of our price range.

"If only we had a little more money," I said to our real estate agent as she drove us down yet another street of homes we couldn't afford. "Even an extra twenty thousand dollars might make a difference."

"Everyone says that, Jodie," she replied. "I have people looking at million-dollar homes who wish they had an extra hundred thousand or so. It doesn't matter what your price range is; everyone feels like they need just a little bit more."

If the woman thought she was consoling me, she wasn't. Robbie and I had been married for eight years, during which time we'd lived in four different rental properties, not including the eighteen months we spent living with my parents (which was before boomerang kids became a thing), where we slept in the room above their garage on a mattress on the floor. We'd checked all the commonsense "before you buy" boxes that financial experts talk about: be married for more than a year, stay out of debt, have three to six months' worth of living expenses in savings, and so on. All of our friends had already purchased their

---

2. You'll find this 25 percent guideline and other home-buying tips in Dave Ramsey's book *The Total Money Makeover: A Proven Plan for Financial Fitness* (Nashville: Nelson, 2013).

first home, and with two children (and hopes for more), I was ready to start nesting in a place of our own.

Eventually, Robbie and I did buy a home. It wasn't pretty, but it was in a good location, fit our budget, and came with some wonderful neighbors. And in the interest of trying to live happily ever after, I repressed all of our painful house-hunting memories—until I got a call from my friend Bonnie. "Will you please pray for Davis and Shelby?" she asked. "They really want to buy a house, but it seems like every time they find a place they like, something goes wrong."

Davis is Bonnie's son. He and his wife, Shelby, had only been married a year, but they were eager to start a family, and the small condominium that Davis had purchased as a young bachelor already felt tight. It made sense, they thought, to start looking for a place with an extra bedroom; ideally, they wanted a house.

"We'll need to sell the condo first," Davis said, "to make it work with our budget. But that shouldn't be hard; the market is up and everyone says that selling is a quick and easy process."

Sure enough, no sooner had they put the condo on the market than they got an offer. It was well below their asking price, and the young couple wrestled with whether to accept it.

"I knew they'd need wisdom," Bonnie told me, "but instead of butting in with my own advice or opinions, I relied on verses like Proverbs 2:6 and James 1:5 and asked God to provide it. And since Davis was maturing into his role as a husband, I covered him with a prayer out of Luke 2:52, that he would grow in wisdom and stature, and in favor with God and man."

═══════════ *Prayer Principle* ═══════════

Asking God to give your child wisdom is always
a good starting place for prayer.

Davis and Shelby decided not to accept the offer—a decision that was validated when they got another contract within the week. This one was for the full asking price, and the couple began packing their things. Bonnie and her husband had a place over their garage (with an actual bed instead of just a mattress on the floor!), and the plan was for Davis and Shelby to move in there for a month or so while they looked for their own home.

With just days to go before closing and the vacant condo in perfect move-in condition, Davis and Shelby got some bad news. The buyer hadn't been able to get his financing approved, and the closing was off.

Frustrated but knowing it couldn't be helped, they put the condo back on the market. A month later, they had a third offer—this time from a buyer who said he had cash. Davis wondered if the offer was too good to be true. Sure enough, just twenty days into the thirty-day "due diligence" period, he and Shelby got a text from the buyer's agent. "Circumstances have changed," the message read. "My client will forfeit his earnest money, as he will not be buying your property."

Davis and Shelby were confused; wasn't this process supposed to be quick and easy? Shelby didn't know a whole lot of Bible verses by heart, but the first one she had ever memorized kept coming to mind: "Trust in the LORD with all your heart, and lean not on your own understanding; in all your ways submit to him, and he will make your paths straight."[3] She and Davis certainly were not leaning on their own understanding—nobody, she figured, could understand this convoluted process. "Help us to trust you, God," she prayed. "And please bring the right buyer along."

Five months and yet another failed contract later, Davis and Shelby were still living above Bonnie's garage.

"I began praying every 'help me' prayer I could find on their behalf," Bonnie confided, "from Psalm 28:6, that God would hear their cry for mercy, to 2 Samuel 22:7, which talks about God hearing us when we are in distress. I don't mean to sound overly dramatic, but they were starting to get seriously discouraged, and I didn't want their young relationship to have to endure the uncertainty—not to mention the living-with-your-in-laws thing—for much longer."

Davis and Shelby put the condo on the market a fourth time. Two days later, they received—and accepted—a very strong offer. Finally, the condo was sold. Relieved—and flush with the cash

---

3. Proverbs 3:5–6.

from the sale—the young couple began house hunting in earnest. This, they figured, would be the fun part.

What they hadn't counted on, though, was the pressure they'd face in what was clearly a seller's market. Homes sold in days, sometimes even in hours. Shelby would find a house she liked and say she wanted to bring her husband to see it, only to have it sold by the time he got off work. The couple wound up making offers on five different properties, even getting in bidding wars with other buyers, and they lost them all.

"The pressure was incredible," Davis said. "We lost one house on Easter Sunday after our agent told us it was 'now or never' and we couldn't increase our bid fast enough. If it hadn't been so stressful, it might have been funny, because we were praying about whether to buy these houses—and telling God we needed his answer in an hour!"

It wasn't funny, though. The process began taking its toll on the newlyweds, who had now been living with Bonnie for almost seven months. All of their belongings were in storage; they had no place to entertain or hang out with friends; and the cross-town commute—often as long as forty-five minutes—meant that Shelby had to leave home at 4:45 a.m. to get to work on time. She wanted to honor her husband, but as Shelby watched one house after another slip away—houses she had fallen in love with—she found herself wondering if maybe Davis was being too conservative in his estimate of how much they could spend. Was it really all that bad if they had to stretch a little?

"I know how hard it was on Shelby," Davis said, "and I wanted to make her happy more than anything. She would find a home and get emotionally attached, even picturing where our furniture would go in the various rooms, and then the bidding war would start, and the price would jump out of our reach."

Shelby's father weighed in. "When you ask God for something," he said, "he will answer in one of three ways. He will say yes, no, or not yet. In the same way that the two of you have to learn to trust each other, you have to learn to trust God and his timing. Right now, it looks like he is telling you to wait and see what he has planned."

Eager as she was to see Davis and Shelby find a home of their own, Bonnie understood this need for patience. "I started praying verses that had to do with waiting well," she said. "The Bible says that God is good to those who hope in him and seek him, and that it is good to wait quietly for the salvation of the Lord.[4] I know this is true—but I also know how hard it is to wait, particularly if you are living in a small place with no privacy and your mother-in-law just downstairs."

Finally, nearly nine months into the process, Shelby found a home she thought was perfect. It was on a corner lot in a cul-de-sac in a neighborhood full of young families (including Davis's brother and his wife, who had become one of Shelby's closest friends), and it had plenty of space for their own family

---

4. Lamentations 3:25–26.

to grow. Bonnie agreed that the house was ideal. But she knew that appearances could be deceiving. "What's wrong with this house?" she asked the listing agent.

"Absolutely nothing," the woman replied, "other than the fact that it's just a little bit out of their price range."

Bonnie wondered whether she and her husband should step in with financial help. They knew Davis had made money on the condo, and their sense was that he and Shelby should be able to handle the home purchase on their own. Plus, they didn't want to make the mistake made by some of their peers who had helped adult children buy homes in pricier neighborhoods. The house, as it sometimes turned out, was just the tip of the iceberg. If the kids were to fit in with their neighbors, suddenly things like nice cars, swim or tennis club memberships, and even private schools became part of the "must-have" picture. Better, Bonnie figured, to let Davis and Shelby forge their own financial path at a pace they could afford.

Prayer Principle

Sometimes the best way to help our adult children isn't to give them money or even advice; it's simply to pray.

Davis was as captivated by the home as Shelby was and—in a move that Bonnie saw as an answer to her prayers about him growing in wisdom—he decided that he and Shelby should meet with an independent financial adviser (someone other than their parents), who could assess their financial situation and make a recommendation about their housing budget. As a result, two things happened. The good news was that the adviser told them they could safely exceed their budgeted amount. The bad news was that during the time it took her to reach that conclusion, the bidding war escalated, and another buyer got the house.

Two weeks later, though, that deal fell through, and the owners offered the home to Davis and Shelby—at a $25,000 discount.

"God heard their cry," Bonnie said, "and he brought them to a beautiful place. Proverbs 16:9 says, 'In their hearts humans plan their course, but the LORD establishes their steps.' I don't know why the process took so long, but I know that God has established them in their home, and we are grateful."

Poised for Prayer

Looking back over their real estate journey, Davis and Shelby marvel over the many ways God ordered their steps. What they saw as a series of derailed plans turned out to be a feast of blessings: The time spent above the garage cemented Shelby's relationship with her in-laws. It allowed the newlyweds to pad their savings. It gave Bonnie a chance to pray strategically for the couple's specific housing needs, as well as for their marriage as they adjusted to their roles as husband and wife.

Shelby and Davis's waiting season tested—and strengthened—

their marriage in ways that many newlyweds don't get to experience. "We were both growing in our relationship with the Lord and in our willingness to depend on him and trust his timing," Shelby said. "And at the same time, I learned that I could also trust my husband."

"And we both learned a lot about how we should make decisions," Davis added. "We have wonderful parents and it's great to have their input, but this process taught me that I needed to put Shelby ahead of my folks. That sounds like a no-brainer, but it's something I guess a lot of young couples take a while to learn. It wasn't painless, but I'm glad we could learn to trust each other in what turned out to be a fairly safe training ground."

Listening to Davis and Shelby share the ups and downs of their home-buying story, I was reminded of what Timothy Keller says about asking God to give us things or do things for us. "We have the assurance that God, our heavenly Father, always wants the best for his children," Keller writes. As a result, we can pray with confidence, knowing that "God will either give us what we ask or give us what we would have asked if we knew everything he knew."[5]

As we pray for our children to find a good place to live, when it feels like God is saying no or not yet, let's not give in to worry or despair. Instead, let's rejoice, knowing that he wants what's best for us and that he is working on giving us (and our kids) the very home we would have asked him for if we had only known.

---

5. Timothy Keller, *Prayer: Experiencing Awe and Intimacy with God* (New York: Penguin, 2014), 228.

Prayers You Can Use

For Yourself

Heavenly Father . . .

As I trust you with _____'s home, thank you for your promise that your people will live in peaceful dwelling places, in secure homes, in undisturbed places of rest.

ISAIAH 32:18

Help me to provide for my children's housing needs, knowing when (and if) I should provide financial help and how best to offer the more valuable shelter of wisdom.

ECCLESIASTES 7:12

When I am tempted to step in with advice or financial help, give me the ability to be still and wait patiently for you.

PSALM 37:7

For Your Children

Heavenly Father . . .

You know exactly when and where _____ should live. Lead him to that appointed place.   ACTS 17:26

Be the builder of _____'s home, her relationship with you, and (if she is married) her relationship with her husband. Unless you build these things, she will labor in vain.

PSALM 127:1

As _____ buys a home, particularly if it needs a lot of improvements, help him do the work. Give him the wisdom and ability to raise up age-old foundations and repair broken walls.

ISAIAH 58:12

Go before _____ and guard her way as she looks for a place to live. Bring her to the place you have prepared.

EXODUS 23:20

Provide _____ with a peaceful dwelling place, one where he can enjoy security and undisturbed periods of rest.

ISAIAH 32:18

Command your blessing on _____'s home and on everything she puts her hand to. Bless her in the land you are giving her.

DEUTERONOMY 28:8

Whether _____ is trying to rent, sell, or buy a home, help him to wait for you; let him be strong and take heart and wait for you.

PSALM 27:14

Give _____ the financial wisdom to budget wisely; let her sit down and estimate the cost before renting or buying a home, so that the process will be able to be completed.

LUKE 14:28

Provide a place for _____ and plant him, so that he can have a home of his own and no longer be disturbed.

2 SAMUEL 7:10

Even as the sparrow and the swallow find their own nests, may _____ find a place to live, and may she long to be near you.   PSALM 84:3

As _____ looks for an earthly home, may his greatest desire be to dwell in your house, to gaze on your beauty, and to seek you.   PSALM 27:4

As _____ looks for a good place to live, remind her that homes are built by wisdom, established by understanding, and beautifully decorated by knowledge.

PROVERBS 24:3–4

CHAPTER 10

Praying for a Job

I will instruct you and teach you in
the way you should go;
I will counsel you with my
loving eye on you.

PSALM 32:8

I can't tell you how many parents, when they heard I was working on this book, let me know they had a story to share. I was excited to interview them, but I had to laugh when I realized that at least two-thirds of the stories were variations on the same theme: praying for your child to get a job. Everyone who has ever had an adult child has, apparently, been down this sometimes long and winding road.

One mom told me how frustrated she had become after her son batted away one job lead after another, since they just didn't seem to fit his "work/life balance." (I thought she was kidding, but then I found out it's a real thing, that today's graduates really are looking for jobs that come complete with a gym membership, Friday happy hours, and even—since I guess they are waiting longer to have children—things like health insurance for their pets. Seriously.)

Another said her daughter didn't want to work "in a cubicle, like Dad."

And a third shared her son's Goldilocks-style journey through everything from starting a business to playing in a rock band, until (and I think this is a brilliant idea) her husband invited a group of older men to serve as an advisory board in the young man's life—a move that ultimately opened the door to a "just right" career in television.

I'd go on, but you get the idea. Plenty of kids need to figure out what to do with their lives, and plenty of parents are praying.

And I'll admit it. I didn't expect to have to pray so hard about my own kids' jobs—and I said as much to author Paula Rinehart when the two of us had lunch together one day. I'd just finished reading her *Strong Women, Soft Hearts*, and I'd loved what she'd said about trust.

"Trust," Paula had written, "hangs somewhere between knowing what your heart longs for and trying to dictate the shape or timing or outcome of your heart's desire. It lies in the willingness to accept the particulars of how and when and where God chooses to intervene. It waits in the cool shade of surrender."[1]

The cool shade of surrender. I liked that image, but I was

---

1. Paula Rinehart, *Strong Women, Soft Hearts: A Woman's Guide to Cultivating a Wise Heart and a Passionate Life* (Nashville: Nelson, 2001), 75.

nowhere near to experiencing it. Instead, I was working up a sweat over things like timing and outcomes in Hillary's life.

"Hillary doesn't have a job," I confided over lunch. "She is back home and living in her bedroom—she's one of those boomerang kids—and she seems *content*."

"She only graduated three months ago," Paula countered. "Trust me; she is probably not content. She's an engineer—they think in linear terms. She is pursuing a job; she's just not doing it the way you would."

Well, she had that one right. Hillary was definitely not looking for a job the way I would have. I would have loaded my résumé into the barrel of a shotgun and pulled the trigger, splattering my education and experience all over any company that was hiring. But Hillary was a little more particular. She graduated with a degree in mechanical and aerospace engineering, and she wanted to be an astronaut. It was a dream she had since the fifth grade, and if she couldn't actually wear a space suit, she at least wanted to do something with rockets.

At first, I shared Hillary's enthusiasm. "Provide the job you have ordained for her," I wrote in my prayer journal. "Fill her life so full of blessing that she will not be able to contain it! Let her joy be complete."[2]

That's a good, biblically based prayer for any new graduate. And I wish I could say that my positive attitude continued, and

---

2. A prayer based on God's promises in Psalm 139:16; Malachi 3:10; John 15:11.

that I had the faith to believe that God puts desires in our hearts that he wants to fulfill. (He does. Psalm 37:4. I'm just saying I wish I would have had the faith to truly believe that.)

I wish I could say I had taken Paula's words to heart and waited in "the cool shade of surrender."

And I wish I could tell you I stood by my daughter, loving her and supporting her and letting her live at home with us, rent-free, as spring rolled into summer, and summer turned to fall, never once resenting the fact that she had polished off the last of the Starbucks K-Cups.

But I didn't. I didn't do any of the good-mother things I should have.

Prayer Principle

If we want to pray with faith, we must anchor our requests in God's promises.

Instead, I spent the better part of a year grappling with fear, frustration, and even anger. And if that's where you are in your own child's job-hunting season, can I just say this one thing? Don't beat yourself up. Give your worries to God, and remember that his grace is sufficient to cover all your mistakes, and his power is made perfect in your weakness.[3] Hold on to

---

3. 2 Corinthians 12:9.

that promise—and to others—because when discouragement and fear try to creep in and cripple our confidence, the Bible is the anchor for our hope. I like how author and prayer expert R. A. Torrey put it: "If I am to have faith when I pray, I must find some promise in the Word of God on which to rest my faith."[4]

I hesitate to tell this story (it does not make me look good), but since we're all in this parenting thing together, I'll go ahead. Maybe you'll find some helpful prayer prompts. Or maybe you'll just read it and be glad you're not me. Either way, here goes!

I was really proud of Hillary for academic accomplishments (she had gotten an A+ in Spacecraft Design), and I looked forward to seeing how God would use her education in the real world. But then, as one after another of her peers landed jobs with important-sounding companies, I felt the first crack in my confidence. Had she missed the hiring window? Were there no space-ish jobs to be had? Or maybe it was the reverse. Hillary would be the first to admit that decision making is not her strong suit, and I began to fear that she hadn't gotten a job because maybe there were just too many interesting choices. The ink on her diploma was still wet, and I was already starting to panic. "Don't you realize how late it is?" I cried out to God. "Don't you think it's time to step in and do something?"

I knew I was being a little dramatic, but I was also conscious of a nagging fear that I had somehow failed as a mother. Had

---

4. R. A. Torrey, *How to Pray* (Chicago: Moody, 1960), 50.

I done something to create a lack of urgency in Hillary? Had I made her tentative or insecure? Or at the other extreme, was I being too pushy? Would it all backfire?

In the midst of my emotional hurricane, I sensed God's rebuke. "Quiet!" he said. "Be still!"[5] It was the same thing he said to the disciples in the boat one stormy night, and I felt my own winds of fear subside. I began to pray that Hillary would also be attentive to his voice.

"Be Hillary's shepherd," I asked, borrowing from John 10:2–4. "May she hear your voice as you call her by name. Lead her into the grown-up world, and may she follow you."

A month went by, during which friends offered suggestions about jobs that Hillary might want to do or cities where she might want to live. "May Hillary be willing to listen to advice and be humble, so that you will guide her and teach her," I prayed.[6] And even though I knew this was a promise given to the Israelites (and that contemporary Christians who claimed it did so knowing that it pertained more to spiritual and eternal blessings than to things like good health, good wealth, and good jobs), I pulled out Jeremiah 29:11. "I know you have plans to prosper Hillary, to give her hope and a future," I prayed, "and I am so grateful for that. But I would also love it if part of your long-term plans for blessing my girl could include a here-and-now job."

July rolled around. Hillary kept researching space companies

---

5. Mark 4:39.
6. Proverbs 12:15; Psalm 25:9.

and looking at job postings, but it didn't seem (to me, anyway) like she was making much progress. I searched the Scriptures for something—anything—that would help me cope with the chasm between my plan ("Just get a job!") and Hillary's ("I want to be an astronaut!"), and I came upon Proverbs 16:9 (NLT): "We can make our plans, but the LORD determines our steps." I realized that it didn't matter whose plan we were following; the outcome was up to the Lord. My job was to get out of his way.

=== *Prayer Principle* ===

We can make all the plans we want—and so can our kids—but God is the one who directs our path.

That acknowledgment was my first step toward the cool shade of surrender. And the next thing I knew, Hillary had taken a job.

As a surf instructor.

To Hillary, the surf job (which was at a camp where she worked in previous summers) seemed like the perfect way to earn an income while she continued to send out résumés. To me, it looked like she was procrastinating, like she was looking for a way to avoid growing up and having to wear shoes every day. And then another worry entered my mind. Surf camp was a place where Hillary clearly fit in; maybe she didn't know if she belonged in the space program. Was she secretly as anxious as I was? I didn't know.

I kept on praying that God would show her where to go, career-wise, using verses like Psalm 32:8 as the basis for my prayers: "Instruct Hillary and teach her the way she should go; counsel her and watch over her." But I also began to pray for her spirit, writing words just like this in my journal:

> *Give Hillary a sense of BELONGING. Let her know she is CHOSEN.*[7]
> *Give Hillary a sense of WORTH. Remind her that she is YOUR WORKMANSHIP, and that you have prepared GOOD WORKS for her to do.*[8]
> *Give Hillary a sense of PURPOSE and IDENTITY as your child, and fill her soul with the knowledge that she is VALUABLE and PRECIOUS and USEFUL to you.*[9]

I prayed this way for nearly two months. And when Hillary came home from the surf camp, two job prospects were waiting.

The first was from a winegrower in California who wanted her to design a new way of processing grapes. That sounded good to me, but it didn't appeal to my girl.

The second was with a structural engineering firm, but when Hillary went for the interview and the guy (who seemed a little

---

7. Ephesians 2:19; Isaiah 41:9; Ephesians 1:4.
8. Psalm 139:13; Ephesians 2:10.
9. Romans 8:15–17; Isaiah 62:3.

creepy) asked her to lie down in the middle of an Applebee's and show him how to "pop up" on a surfboard, she balked.

I would have too.

But that didn't prevent me from wishing that Hillary would just let go of the whole astronaut thing. I figured there had to be a million jobs out there for engineers; why did she have to be so single-minded in her focus? "Aim lower" has never been the best motivational speech, but it's pretty much the way I began to think (and speak) about Hillary's job search. I'll spare you the details, but you know the Proverbs 31 mother, the one who "speaks with wisdom, and faithful instruction is on her tongue"? Picture the opposite.

I wrote some fairly frank things in my prayer journal, and I was sure that God would understand, and that (being a parent) he'd take my side. I opened my Bible to give him a chance to respond. And—no kidding—here's what I read:

Gently encourage the stragglers, and reach out for the exhausted, pulling them to their feet. Be patient with each person, attentive to individual needs. And be careful that when you get on each other's nerves you don't snap at each other. Look for the best in each other, and always do your best to bring it out.[10]

10.   1 Thessalonians 5:14–15 MSG.

Okay, then. God wanted me to encourage Hillary with gentleness and patience instead of sarcasm and snapping. Point taken. But he wasn't finished. I read the next few verses:

> Be cheerful no matter what; pray all the time; thank God no matter what happens. This is the way God wants you who belong to Christ Jesus to live.[11]

Was he serious? I could pray, and I could resolve to thank God for whatever it was that he had planned. But . . . be cheerful? I was glad I knew Philippians 2:13 ("It is God who works in you to will and to act in order to fulfill his good purpose"), because if cheerfulness was required to live the way God wanted me to, he was going to have to give me some sort of divine lobotomy.

September crawled by. Since she had time on her hands and an affinity for teenagers, Hillary volunteered to work with Young Life, a ministry to high schoolers. Hillary loved the kids, and they seemed to love her back, and as I watched a sense of purpose and joy begin to bloom again in Hillary's life, I realized that her volunteer work was something I could be thankful for. Maybe even cheerful about.

In October, a neighbor arranged for Hillary to take a tour of NASA Langley Research Center, which is about forty minutes from our home. Hillary was captivated. She loved the designs

---

11. 1 Thessalonians 5:16–18 MSG.

and projects she saw, and even better, she could understand how everything worked.

But NASA didn't have any job openings, so Hillary began making plans to go to Brazil, where she had done volunteer work during her college spring breaks. The orphanage where she had helped out was opening a trade school; Hillary figured she could teach welding or some other engineering-related job skill.

Then she got a phone call. Could she come to NASA for an interview the next day? A post had just opened up—one designed to be filled by a young engineer—and someone she had met on her tour remembered her name.

Flustered—and giddy—Hillary put Brazil on hold and began planning her interview wardrobe. I wasn't sure how a rocket scientist was supposed to dress, so I left her staring at her closet and dug out my Bible. I'd moved into Daniel by then, where I found a gold mine of prayer prompts:

- Cause the officials at NASA to show favor and sympathy to Hillary.[12]
- Give her knowledge and understanding, and may she speak with wisdom and tact.[13]
- Let Hillary have a keen mind and the ability to explain riddles and solve difficult problems.[14]

---

12. Daniel 1:9.
13. Daniel 1:17; 2:14.
14. Daniel 5:12.

She went for the interview and loved it. But then a couple of weeks went by with no word. Hillary took NASA's silence in stride, figuring it might take a while for them to interview other candidates, but I was worried. Had God forgotten my girl? Had the whole thing just been a big tease?

I opened my Bible to Nehemiah 9, the part where the Israelites show up in sackcloth and ashes and confess their sins. I could relate.

"Lord," I prayed, "I am sad and I'm hurt. I thought I knew you and how you would work in answer to our hopes and our prayers. I thought you had put the desire to work at NASA in Hillary's heart and that you would fulfill that desire.

"But maybe I haven't really trusted you. Maybe I've been focused on your provision for Hillary's life, finding my joy in that *outcome* rather than finding my joy in *you*. I confess that I have been controlling, self-centered, and driven by fear. I've questioned Hillary's approach to job hunting, and I've questioned yours.

"I am sorry for my arrogance. Please give me your grace."

There it was. The cool shade of surrender. Hillary's dream job was within sight—but after eight months of wrestling in prayer on her behalf, I was willing to let it go.

I sat there, staring at my open Bible. "Stand up and praise the LORD your God, who is from everlasting to everlasting."[15] That was what the priests told the Israelites to do, once they finished their confession. Even though I felt about as big as a worm

---

15. Nehemiah 9:5.

(and like the *last* thing God might want was to hear anything more out of me), I figured I ought to join them.

So I did. I began to praise God for his faithfulness, for the way he walked alongside our family through the job-hunting journey, and for the provision he had given us in his Word. Nothing had changed outwardly—Hillary still had no job—but in the shade of surrender, that didn't matter so much anymore.

And then my eye fell on Nehemiah 9:8: "You have kept your promise because you are righteous."

You can probably guess what happened. Two weeks later, NASA called again. Hillary was ordering chicken nuggets with her Young Life girls when her phone rang, so she put the space people on hold. (Did I mention that she doesn't always do things the way her uptight mother would?) Anyhow, they offered her the job, and she took it.

Poised for Prayer

Why did it take eight months for Hillary to get a job? Or to put it another way, why did it take me eight months to pry my controlling fingers off of her life and surrender to God? I don't know. But God does. And as Priscilla Shirer teaches in her *Discerning the Voice of God*, "The purposes of God not only involve specific plans; they also involve specific timing."[16]

---

16. Priscilla Shirer, *Discerning the Voice of God: How to Recognize When God Is Speaking*, rev. ed. (Chicago: Moody, 2012), 172.

> Trusting God with our children's future means
> being willing to trust his timing.

Had God provided Hillary's job when I wanted him to—the day she graduated from college—she would have missed the opportunity to work with Young Life, a volunteer post she loved. She's still passionate about engineering, but as she told me just the other day, the chance to invest in the lives of young girls has been more satisfying than anything she could have imagined.

Not only that, but had she gone straight into the workforce after graduation, she might have missed the opportunity to meet (and then fall in love with) her husband, who brought a group of guys on the same Young Life ski trip where Hillary showed up with her crew of young girls.

God's agenda is always so much bigger than ours. My prayer for Hillary's job was about her finding employment; his answer was about teaching me to relax, to wait in the cool shade of surrender, and to realize that what Hillary and I really needed—and what God wanted to give us—was more of himself.

Prayers You Can Use

For Yourself

Heavenly Father . . .

Thank you that there is an appointed time for everything. Help me to be still before you and to wait patiently on your perfect timing.   ECCLESIASTES 3:1; PSALM 37:7

Help me get along with my child. Show me how to gently encourage her, pulling her to her feet as she looks for a job. Let me be patient and attentive to her needs. When we get on one another's nerves, keep us from snapping at each other; rather help me to look for the best in her and bring it out.   1 THESSALONIANS 5:14–15 MSG

Let my desire be not just for the gift of a job or a career, but for the greater gift of your presence. Let this be my cry: Whom have I in heaven but you? And earth has nothing I desire besides you.   PSALM 73:25

For Your Children

Heavenly Father . . .

May your favor rest on _____ . Establish the work of his hands, and make his efforts successful.

PSALM 90:17 NIV, NLT

Give _____ success by granting her favor in the presence of potential employers. NEHEMIAH 1:11

Remind _____ that he is your handiwork, created to do good works, which you prepared in advance for him to do. EPHESIANS 2:10

Let _____ have aptitude for every kind of learning. Cause her to be well informed, quick to understand, and qualified to serve in the job you set before her.

DANIEL 1:4

When _____ interviews for a job, let him speak with wisdom and tact. Give him knowledge and discernment.

DANIEL 2:14, 21

Cause _____ to delight herself in you, and give her the desires of her heart. PSALM 37:4

May _____ be wise in the way he acts toward potential employers. Let him make the most of every opportunity. May his words be always full of grace and seasoned with salt, so that he will know how to answer any question.

COLOSSIANS 4:5–6

Grant _____ the ability to trust in your timing and to be willing to wait to find out what you command concerning what she is to do.   NUMBERS 9:8

Replace _____'s job-hunting anxiety with the comforting knowledge that all the days ordained for him were written in your book before one of them came to be.   PSALM 139:16

Let _____ use whatever gifts she has received to serve others, being a faithful steward of your grace in its various forms.   1 PETER 4:10

In _____'s heart he is planning his course; help him see that you, Lord, determine his steps.   PROVERBS 16:9

Do not let _____ be anxious about anything, but prompt her to pray about everything, bringing her requests to you with thanksgiving. And may your peace, which transcends understanding, guard her heart and her mind in Christ Jesus.   PHILIPPIANS 4:6–7

CHAPTER 11

Praying When Your Children Have Children

I will pour out my Spirit on your offspring,
and my blessing on your descendants.

ISAIAH 44:3

Back when *Praying the Scriptures for Your Children* was released, my mom told me she wished she'd had it as a resource when my siblings and I were growing up. I had two thoughts. The first was that she didn't need a book to help her pray the Scriptures; my mother is one of the most biblically literate and powerful prayer warriors I know.

The second was that I was glad she had the book then, because she was using it to pray for my children. They were ages five through eleven, and at the time, my daily life was a blur of car pools, soccer games, homework, meal prep, and laundry. (And that was before you factored in all my Very Important Jobs, like organizing the hula-hoop competition for the elementary school's annual Bazooka Blowout.) There were plenty of days when I barely had time to throw up a "God, bless Annesley," let alone beseech God to instill in her things like compassion, discernment, or the ability to speak kindly to her siblings.

I had attended a Christian parenting conference where one of the speakers asked, "If you aren't praying for your children, who is?" I know the speaker meant that as a motivational charge, but honestly? I heard her and felt guilty. Even though I'd written a book about praying for your children, I didn't always do a good job of actually *doing* it. I wanted to spend time asking God to fill my kids with wisdom and bless them with godly friendships and all, but it seemed like somebody was always throwing up, falling down, or needing me to make a turkey costume because all of the Pilgrim parts had been taken.

I needed reinforcements. And knowing that my parents were on the job—that they were talking to God about my kids' health and their character and their relationship with Jesus—was an indescribable gift.

My friend Susan understands the value of this gift. She has five married children and twenty-one grandkids. In order to pray for them all, she assigns a day of the week to each family. And knowing she can go where her children sometimes can't ("Grandkids roll their eyes less at grandparents than they do at parents," she says), she doesn't mind letting the younger generation know she is praying, whether it's for a little one's fear of going to sleep-away camp for the first time or an older child's yearning for friends. Even the most unremarkable events—like soccer games or math tests—can become an invitation to pray.

For instance, Susan's grandson Will was a sophomore in high school, facing a particularly challenging exam that could affect his overall GPA and ultimately his college applications. When Susan heard about the test, she asked God to provide things like mental clarity, alertness, and the ability for Will to recall what he had learned and do well—but she didn't tell her grandson all of those details. Instead, when exam day rolled around, she sent him a simple text message: *I am praying for you.*

Afterward, Will was clearly excited. He'd done better than he'd hoped he would, and—whether he was smarter than he thought or the test was just easier than he expected—he figured that having a praying grandma in his corner had to be a plus.

Susan has prayed similar prayers for all of her grandchildren, asking God to provide everything from good health to good time management. "Children are all different," she told me, "but a lot of their needs are the same. They all need safety, wisdom, protection from evil, fellowship opportunities, and godly mates (if they are to marry). They need the sorts of things you wrote about in *Praying the Scriptures for Your Children*. I use those prayers for my grandchildren!"

I was grateful for that endorsement, but I knew I hadn't covered everything in that book. How, for instance, did Susan pray for her own children, now that they'd become parents? (I don't have grandchildren yet, but I want to be ready—and who better to learn from than someone who has been there twenty-one times?)

Susan told me she and her husband, John, began praying for their daughters and daughters-in-law as soon as they learned they were expecting. "John and I prayed Psalm 139 during our kids' pregnancies, asking God to fill them with peace about their unborn babies, knowing that he was forming them and ordaining all of their days—including the day that each child would be born.

"And as our grandchildren entered new phases, from toddler-hood to the teen years, we often prayed that our kids would call out to God for wisdom," she continued. "Nobody really knows how to be a parent, so we asked God to give them a generous helping of wisdom, just as he promised to do."[1]

Sometimes these wisdom prayers get very specific. When John and Susan realized that one of their sons-in-law didn't seem to be connecting well with his son, they asked God for help. "The two guys are wired very differently," Susan said. "I began to ask God to give [the dad] wisdom to take the initiative in the relationship, as well as the creativity to discover some common ground and shared interests with his son."

Knowing that prayer support can be every bit as helpful to a young family as things like meals and babysitting, Susan keeps a notebook that includes specific requests for each grandchild.

---

1. James 1:5.

"I ask my kids how I can pray for their kids," she told me. "That's not a very threatening question; even if your adult children aren't walking with the Lord, they will usually be grateful for a grandparent's love and support. And when we demonstrate love for our grandchildren by showing an interest in their lives, it's like adding glue to our relationship with our own children and their spouses."

Indeed. Susan and John have seen a strengthening of their family ties as the younger parents share concerns over everything from sibling relationships and character development to "nonspiritual" things like finding a soccer team for their daughter to join or a group of friends who share their son's interest in music.

"Johnny and I are delighted when our kids and their spouses ask us to pray about something," Susan said. "But we have to remember to watch our tongues. They are coming to us for prayer—not necessarily for advice."

Prayer Principle

Praying for your grandchildren strengthens your relationship with your children and their spouses.

In addition to supporting their children with prayer, Susan and John also offer a tangible gift of time. Once a grandchild reaches the age of four, he or she is invited to participate in the annual "Cousins Camp" they host each summer.

Cousins Camp builds family relationships through fun and games (anything goes, from laid-back picnics and fishing trips to heated guacamole-making contests and a race through a giant obstacle course). It also gives Susan and John a window into where their grandchildren are, spiritually. "The thing we prayed most for our kids, and now for our grandkids, is that they would come to Christ at a young age," Susan said, "and that they would fall in love with God's Word. The Bible is the only authority and source of wisdom that will never change. Our culture will change; families will change; and parents and grandparents won't always be around to provide direction or stability in a child's life. We want our grandchildren to learn to depend on God's Word as their source of security, instruction, and joy."

To help facilitate this connection, Susan and John give each camper a journal. Tucked inside the back cover is a letter from "Ghee" and "Poppy." In addition to affirming a child's identity and sense of belonging with promises like Psalm 139:14 ("you are wonderfully made") and Hebrews 13:5 ("God will never leave you or forsake you"), the letter offers a simple explanation of salvation: "Going to heaven isn't dependent on being good enough to deserve it," Ghee and Poppy write. "No one is good enough to deserve heaven. This is a gift to those who have accepted that Christ died for their sins."

Susan and John's note also includes some key verses about salvation (e.g., 1 John 1:9; John 1:12; John 3:16), but I think my favorite part of their letter is a paragraph that comes near the end, one that points the children beyond the boundaries of Cousins Camp and into the wider family of Christ:

> You not only have a big family of cousins who love you and love Jesus, but a great, large family of older brothers and sisters in Christ who will help you grow up in Him. Just as all of us go through different physical growth stages, you will go through different stages in your spiritual growth. It's so important to have friends to whom you can go with your spiritual questions. There is no question or doubt or feeling that is silly or insignificant. And it really helps to have others who have "been there" to guide you on the way! You can always ask an older Christian any questions you have. They will be glad to help you.

I love this paragraph for several reasons. First, I like the way that Susan and John point their grandchildren toward older believers. At Cousins Camp, the young initiates have the opportunity to partner with an older cousin, one who will pray with them and help them craft what, even at a tender age, is best described as their "testimony." I didn't have an older cousin to show me the spiritual ropes, but I did have friends who were older—both chronologically and in their relationships with Christ—and even now, forty-plus years later, I remain grateful for the way these peers modeled and explained God's grace in ways I could understand. No matter whether it's a cousin, sibling, or friend, the importance of this type of mentorship in a child's life cannot be overstated.

Second, I love how Susan and John's words underscore a sense of belonging.

=== *Prayer Principle* ===

Ask God to provide friends and mentors who will lovingly point your grandchildren toward Christ.

It doesn't matter if our natural family is large or small or even whether or not our relatives are walking with the Lord. When we ask Jesus to be our Savior and our Lord, we gain a permanent place in the family of Christ, and we can all share in the promises that Susan and John wrote out for their crew. If your adult children do not have a vibrant Christian faith or if their family has been fractured by divorce, sickness, or death, don't let that be a spiritual obstacle for your grandchildren. Instead, take every opportunity you can to remind them that they are part of a bigger family, one where they will always have a place and where nothing can separate them from their heavenly Father's love.

And finally, I appreciate Susan and John's sensitivity toward the various stages of spiritual growth that their grandchildren will experience. It's important for those of us who are praying grandparents to remember that our children and their spouses might hit some rocky patches in their own faith. Instead of worrying that our grandchildren won't be "raised right," we can take these concerns to God in prayer. Instead of always speaking up when our children don't parent the way we would (they let their son listen to that music; they let their daughter wear that shirt; they don't place a priority on family dinners or whatever), we can talk to God and ask him to have his way in their lives (and in ours). There will, of course, be times when we feel compelled to step in or offer advice (because, after all, you never stop being a parent), but I appreciate Susan's time-tested counsel: "When in doubt, don't say anything. Just pray."

===================== *Prayer Principle* =====================

> If you have concerns about your grandchildren
> or how they are being raised, take your worries
> to God and give his grace time to work.

Being a grandparent—praying for your children and your grandchildren—comes with what Susan calls a "relaxed joy." You don't always see the day-in and day-out struggles a child may be facing, and you are not responsible (the way a parent is) for handling or responding to those things. But that doesn't mean it's always easy. In the same way that parents can fall prey to insecurity or doubt, Susan cautions grandparents against falling into the "comparison trap."

You might, for example, feel inadequate because you've

never thought about writing your grandchildren a spiritually encouraging letter, let alone hosting a camp! But Susan battles her own feelings of inadequacy. She cannot, for example, shop for, wrap, and mail birthday and Christmas gifts for all of her grandchildren—let alone afford to get them all the latest electronic gadgets or must-have clothing she sees some of her peers buying—so she just sends a (small) check in a card every year.

"And that's just the beginning," Susan confesses. "One of my friends regularly Skypes and FaceTimes with her grandchildren. I have no idea what that stuff even is; I can barely check my own email. But here's the thing I need to keep telling myself: We can't worry about what other grandparents are doing, and we can't look to our grandchildren for affirmation or approval. Just like we need to pray that *their* identity is firmly rooted in Christ, we need to be sure that *ours* is too. That's the only way we'll do the things that God wants us to do—the things that we *can* do—and avoid the comparison trap. That's the only way we'll really be able to get rid of silly distractions and pray effectively for our grandchildren."

Poised for Prayer

Like I said, I don't have grandchildren yet. But I am really looking forward to the day when I do, and I am already collecting God's promises for that season.

"Children's children are a crown to the aged," reads Proverbs

17:6. Or how about this encouraging word from Proverbs 16:31? "Gray hair is a crown of splendor." And think about Job. He had a rough go of it, for sure, but "the LORD blessed the latter part of Job's life more than the former part . . . he saw his children and their children to the fourth generation."[2]

Clearly, we've still got some good years ahead. Let's use them well.

If you prayed the Scriptures for your own children when they were young, you know the satisfaction that comes with tapping into the Bible's promises, knowing that your words are being spoken in accordance with God's will. If you're new to the whole Scripture-prayer thing, what better way to start blessing your adult children than to stand in the gap for them now?[3] Your grown-up children who are moms and dads are probably trying to get the grass stains out of the soccer shorts, or they're at the pediatrician's office with the third case of strep throat this year. Let your kids know you are praying for their kids—and for them. They'll be grateful.

This may be particularly true if your child is a single parent. He or she may be feeling lonely, overwhelmed, or even just too exhausted or distracted to pray. Knowing you are on the job—that you are standing in the gap as an advocate on their

---

2. Job 42:12, 16.
3. "Standing in the gap" is a reference to Ezekiel 22:30, where Scripture seems to indicate that God sometimes waits on our prayers before he acts and that he actually looks for people who will pray.

behalf—can provide tremendous emotional comfort and relief. Parenting is hard work; it helps to know you are not alone.

There are, obviously, hundreds of prayers you can pray for your grandchildren. I've pulled a collection of my favorites from *Praying the Scriptures for Your Children* and *Praying the Scriptures for Your Teens* and included them at the end of this chapter. You can also get weekly prayer verses delivered via email at jodieberndt.com, although if you're like Susan—or me—you might need to ask one of your tech-savvy grandkids to get you signed up.

In the meantime, here's my prayer for you as you look forward to (or enjoy) being a grandparent: "May you still bear fruit in old age; may you stay fresh and green. May the Lord continually bless you, and may you live to enjoy your children's children."[4]

---

4. Psalm 92:14 NLT; Psalm 128:3–6 NLT.

Prayers You Can Use

For Yourself

Heavenly Father . . .

May your love remain with me forever as I fear you; may your salvation extend to my children's children.

PSALM 103:17 NLT

May I never forget your laws and the good things you have done; equip me to teach them to my children and grandchildren.   DEUTERONOMY 4:9

Be with me even when I am old and gray; let me declare your power to the next generation and your mighty acts to all who are to come.   PSALM 71:18

For Your Children (as They Parent)

Heavenly Father . . .

Equip _____ to start their children off in the way they should go.   PROVERBS 22:6

Help _____ not to exasperate his children but to bring them up in the training and instruction that you value.

EPHESIANS 6:4

When _____ needs parenting wisdom, prompt him to ask you for it, and give it generously to him.   JAMES 1:5

Thank you for your promise to gently lead those that have young; please lead _____ as she raises her children.

ISAIAH 40:11

(For a single parent) Let _____ know they are not alone. Remind them that you will never leave them, that you will strengthen them, and that you are always praying for them and for their children.

DEUTERONOMY 31:6; ISAIAH 41:10;
ROMANS 8:34

For Your Grandchildren

Heavenly Father . . .

Put people in _____'s life who will gently instruct him, and give him repentance leading to a knowledge of the truth.   2 TIMOTHY 2:25

Open _____'s eyes and turn her from darkness to light and from the power of Satan to God, so that she may receive forgiveness of sins and a place among those who are sanctified by faith in Christ.   ACTS 26:18

Make your word a lamp to _____'s feet and a light for his path.   PSALM 119:105

Clothe _____ with compassion, kindness, gentleness, humility, and patience.   COLOSSIANS 3:12

Let _____ take refuge in you and be glad; let her ever sing for joy. Spread your protection over _____ that she may rejoice in you.   PSALM 5:11

Keep _____ from all harm. Watch over his life; watch over his coming and going, both now and forevermore.

PSALM 121:7–8

May _____ grow as Jesus did, in wisdom and stature and in favor with God and man.   LUKE 2:52

Let _____ flee the evil desires of youth and pursue righteousness, faith, love, and peace; let her enjoy the company of those who call on you out of a pure heart.

2 TIMOTHY 2:22

Cause _____ to obey and honor his parents, so that it may go well with him and that he may enjoy a long life.

 EPHESIANS 6:1–3

Work in _____ to think and act according to your good purpose. PHILIPPIANS 2:13

Enable _____ to be strong and courageous. Don't let him get frightened or discouraged, but let him know you will be with him wherever he goes. JOSHUA 1:9

Teach _____ what is best for her and direct her in the way she should go. ISAIAH 48:17

PART 4

PRAYING
for Your ADULT
CHILD'S *Health,
Safety, and
Well-Being*

CHAPTER 12

Praying through a Health Crisis

This is what the LORD ... says: I have heard your prayer and seen your tears; I will heal you.

2 KINGS 20:5

Leslie pushed her way through the hospital's double doors, searching for her son-in-law's familiar face. She had jumped in the car as soon as she got Sam's phone call; now, more than three hours and two hundred miles later, Leslie was desperate for news. Was her daughter, Jenny, still alive?

Just forty-eight years old, Jenny had suffered what doctors were calling a "massive stroke." Leslie hadn't gotten many details—or at least she hadn't been able to process them—other than the devastating news that Jenny's brain was bleeding badly and that back-to-back surgeries had not been able to reduce the swelling. Driving down the highway, the familiar words from Isaiah 41:10 came again and again to Leslie's mind: "Do not fear, for I am with you; do not be dismayed, for I am your God.

I will strengthen you and help you; I will uphold you with my righteous right hand."

"Uphold Jenny," Leslie prayed. "Strengthen her and help her. Protect us all from fear. Be with us."

How many times had she prayed prayers just like that one during her fifty-two years of motherhood? Leslie had lost count. From cradling a baby and waiting for the fever to break, to rushing a child to the emergency room after a sports injury, to sleepless nights waiting for a teen to get home safely, Leslie was no stranger to worry and fear. This time, though, it felt different. Never before had a child's very life been on the line. Never before had she felt so utterly helpless. Leslie didn't want to be afraid, but she couldn't help it. She was.

Rounding a corner, she caught sight of Sam at the end of a corridor, his six-foot-two-inch frame slumped against the hospital wall. He saw Leslie and straightened up, extending his arms. Leslie felt the tears coming as she returned the hug. "How is she?" she asked.

"It's not good," Sam replied, his voice breaking. "They asked if I wanted them to try to stop the bleeding one more time, but they didn't sound hopeful. None of the scans look good. But I told them to go ahead. We have to try. Jenny is a competitor; she would want to fight."

Leslie knew what Sam meant. A fitness fanatic and marathon runner, Jenny's gritty determination had contributed to her success in balancing the demands of motherhood (she and Sam had raised two sons) with the challenges of her career; she was among the most highly respected attorneys in Virginia. "I agree," she said. "Thank you."

After what seemed like an eternity, the chief neurosurgeon came out with the news: the third surgery had gone better than anyone expected. Jenny would be moved to the intensive care unit, where she would be kept in a coma to give her brain time to heal. They couldn't speculate on the extent of the damage; only time would tell that.

Leslie knew Jenny wasn't out of the woods—not by a long shot. Closing her eyes, she thought back to one of the Bible stories she learned as a child, the one about Gideon's fleece.[1] "O Lord," she prayed, "please give me a sign. Give me something to know you are with us, that you are with Jenny. I need some assurance that she will not die."

She opened her eyes and looked out the hospital's big plate-glass window. There, on the horizon, was a spectacular pink and purple sunset—and right in the middle of the clouds was a perfectly shaped heart. Leslie felt an inexplicable peace settle over her soul. She didn't know what the future held, but as one of her favorite old gospel songs put it, she knew who held the future.

The weeks that followed were a blur, as one medical procedure gave way to the next. Leslie found herself clinging to verses like 1 John 4:18 ("Perfect love drives out fear") to bolster her

---

1. See Judges 6:36–40.

faith and keep anxiety at bay. Two decompressive craniectomies (which involved removing a sizable portion of Jenny's skull) were performed to deal with the brain swelling, and any number of scary-sounding devices—a ventilator, a shunt, catheters, braces, and PICC lines—were inserted and applied in what Leslie could only trust was a strategic progression toward recovery.

=== *Prayer Principle* ===

Trusting God when we don't know what the
future holds opens the door to peace.

To her untrained eye, it didn't look as though Jenny was getting any better. The chief neurosurgeon had explained the need for patience, but he could not answer Leslie's unspoken questions, the what-ifs that came unbidden in the middle of the night: Would Jenny be able to speak? To smile? Would she ever walk again? The brain bleed had been severe, and Leslie knew enough about stroke victims to realize that when Jenny woke up, there was a chance she would be partially paralyzed, that her memory would be impaired, and that she might not even be able to communicate.

Jenny had been born on Leslie's birthday, August 28. Somewhere along the way, the two women had attached a biblical significance to those numbers—8 and 28—and adopted Romans 8:28 as their favorite verse. Now, the promise became a lifeline:

"And we know that in all things God works for the good of those who love him, who have been called according to his purpose." Surely, God was at work, and he could be counted on to bring good to Jenny, even out of such pain. Leslie had no idea how he might accomplish such a thing, but she continued to cling to the Romans promise, praying that he would.

Finally, after Jenny had been in a coma for three weeks, doctors announced it was time for her to return to consciousness. The tracheostomy tube meant she wouldn't be able to speak, not at first, but they hoped to assess her mental and physical abilities by asking for a simple thumbs-up in answer to some basic questions. As the days passed, things like, "Is your name Jenny?" gave way to trickier queries ("Was Aaron the brother of Moses?"), and it soon became clear that Jenny wanted to move beyond hand gestures.

"Give her a pen and paper," suggested Jenny's sister, Beth.

Unable to move her left arm, Jenny grasped the pen with her right hand and scratched out a message: "Throat hurts."

Throat hurts! Leslie couldn't remember a time when the realization that one of her children was in pain had come as good news, but this development certainly was. Jenny could think clearly; she could feel pain; and she could communicate. And when she eventually used that pen to ask her doctors to explain the progression of her recovery, they were stunned. "That's some pretty serious cognitive thinking," the neurosurgeon said. "This girl will be fine."

This girl will be fine.

Leslie wanted to dance right there in the hospital! It certainly didn't look like Jenny would be fine (she still couldn't move most of her body or speak), but Leslie knew better than to limit her understanding to what she could see. Faith, she knew, was having "confidence in what we hope for and assurance about what we do not see."[2]

Leslie wanted to be like Abraham, the patriarch who, "against all hope," did not waver through unbelief.[3] But as weeks stretched into months, with progress measured in such miniscule victories as the ability to move a toe, weariness set in. The doctors had removed Jenny's ventilator and the tracheostomy tube, paving the way for speech, but from her very first word (a whispered "Mom"), it was clear that conversation would not come easily. Leslie could tell that her daughter, once so accustomed to powering her way through any mental or physical challenge, was struggling with frustration and fear.

For her part, Leslie felt defeated. After a half century of motherhood, she was used to being able to "fix" things or at least make them better. Now, she could do nothing to help. She was mentally and physically fatigued, and she knew that Sam (who had turned a corner of Jenny's hospital room into an office and rarely left his wife's bedside) was in even worse shape. He never complained, but the weeks spent researching rehab facilities,

---

2. Hebrews 11:1.
3. Romans 4:18, 20.

dealing with insurance companies, and sleeping on a too-small recliner in Jenny's room had to be taking a toll. Watching Sam rub Jenny's feet or adjust her pillows, Leslie marveled at her son-in-law's fortitude. She realized she was watching love in action, the kind of love that "always protects, always trusts, always hopes, always perseveres."[4]

One night, after leaving the hospital, Leslie dropped to her knees. "Give us peace and endurance," she prayed. "Let Jenny—let all of us—run with perseverance the race marked out for us. Let us fix our eyes on Jesus, the author and perfecter of our faith, who for the joy set before him endured the cross."

Leslie had lifted a prayer out of Hebrews 12:1–3, and as she thought about the cross that Christ bore, she realized that he was willing to carry Jenny's suffering as well. Mentally, she surrendered her daughter's life—her pain, her recovery, her future—to the Lord. Instead of focusing on the trials that lay ahead, Leslie shifted her thoughts to all that God had already done for their family. He hadn't just preserved Jenny's life; he had shown them a depth of love and compassion they had never fully recognized before. He had given them hope, couched in the promises of his Word. He had provided an incredibly skilled and attentive medical staff. And he had worked through a host of friends and family members to provide tangible blessings—everything from caring for the family

---

4. 1 Corinthians 13:7.

dogs to converting a bathroom in Sam and Jenny's home to be handicap accessible—in preparation for the day when she would finally come home.

===== *Prayer Principle* =====

Sometimes the key to praying with perseverance is simply to stop looking at your problems and focus instead on who God is and what he has already done.

Nearly four months after her stroke, Jenny did come home. Amid the celebration, Leslie's mind went back to one of the first days they had spent in the hospital. Jenny's brother, Wyatt, had found Leslie weeping inconsolably. "Don't cry, Mom," he had said. "God would not have brought Jenny this far, and he wouldn't have performed the first miracle of keeping her alive, if he wasn't prepared to see it through to completion."

"He who began a good work in you will carry it on to completion." Rarely had the promise of Philippians 1:6 carried such power. Likewise, the words from Romans 8:28 (Leslie and Jenny's "birthday" verse) took on added significance once Jenny was finally able to speak again. "I remember waking up from the coma," she had said, "with a powerful sense that I had been covered in prayer. I had no idea what was happening to me, but I was filled with an inexplicable peace, knowing that somehow God was going to work it all out for good."

Poised for Prayer

In the years following Jenny's stroke, Leslie continued to marvel at God's goodness. Her daughter regained strength and mobility, relearning how to walk, cook, and even ride horses! God had done what Leslie, despite all of her maternal instincts and abilities, could not do: he had preserved life, worked healing, and—true to his word—given strength to his people and blessed them with peace.[5]

It doesn't matter what our kids are facing or what our parental worries are, Jesus offers this invitation: "Come to me, all you who are weary and burdened, and I will give you rest."[6] What a beautiful promise, particularly as we pray for our children's health and safety. Jesus wants everyone—Jews and Gentiles, rich and poor, strong believers and those with little faith—to draw near to him. Just look at a few "weary and burdened" moms and dads who came to him with their concerns:

- A synagogue ruler fell at Jesus' feet, begging him to heal his twelve-year-old daughter.
- A Canaanite woman cried out on behalf of her daughter.
- A desperate father whose boy had been tormented by demons "from childhood" asked the Lord to take pity on them—and help him overcome his unbelief.[7]

---

5. Psalm 29:11.
6. Matthew 11:28.
7. Luke 8:41–42; Matthew 15:28; Mark 9:17–24.

===== *Prayer Principle* =====

God doesn't just want to heal your child;
he wants to take care of you too.

In all of these cases (and more), Jesus stepped in to heal. But he didn't just help the sick children; his ministry included words of hope and encouragement for their hurting and weary parents:

- "Don't be afraid," he told the synagogue ruler.
- "Woman, you have great faith," he said to the Canaanite.
- "Everything is possible for one who believes," he promised the long-suffering father of the demon-possessed boy.

Why was Jesus always so tender? Why didn't he just heal with a word or a touch and move on?

I have to believe it is because God is not just interested in results; he wants relationship. He knows how we feel when our children are hurting, and he wants to carry that weight.

The Bible says that Jesus "took up our pain and bore our suffering" and that "the punishment that brought us peace was on him, and by his wounds we are healed."[8] This is an invitation, like the Matthew 11:28 invitation, to give him our burdens, both physical and emotional. In the bigger picture, though, it is an

---

8. Isaiah 53:4–5.

invitation to relationship, a call to enjoy sweet fellowship with the Lord, here on earth and for all eternity.

This same Bible passage in Isaiah, a few verses later, says that when Jesus looked at what his anguish had accomplished, he was "satisfied." To him, all of the pain and suffering he went through on our behalf was worth it.

He took up our pain. He bore our suffering. By his wounds we are healed. Therein lies our invitation to pray, knowing that God is for us and that nothing can ever separate us from his love.[9]

---

9. See Romans 8:31, 38–39.

Prayers You Can Use

For Yourself

Heavenly Father ...

Thank you for telling us we should always pray and not give up. Help me not to become weary as I pray for _____, but to remember that your timing is perfect.

LUKE 18:1; GALATIANS 6:9

May I speak with gracious words that are sweet to the soul and healing to the bones. PROVERBS 16:24

You tell us to confess our sins to each other and pray for each other so that we may be healed, and that the prayer of a righteous person is powerful and effective. Search my heart, remove my sin, and equip me to pray with power.

JAMES 5:16; PSALM 139:23

For Your Child

Heavenly Father ...

Be with _____. Protect him from fear. Strengthen him, help him, and uphold him. ISAIAH 41:10

May _____ praise you in her inmost being, knowing that you forgive all her sins and heal all her diseases.

PSALM 103:1–3

Send out your word and heal _____; rescue him from the grave.   PSALM 107:20

Help _____ not to lose heart. When she feels like she is outwardly wasting away, renew her day by day.

2 CORINTHIANS 4:16

Cause _____ to keep your word in his heart, knowing that it brings life and health to his whole body.

PROVERBS 4:20–22

May _____ enjoy good health, and may all go well with her.   3 JOHN 1:2

Heal _____, Lord, and he will be healed. Save him and he will be saved.   JEREMIAH 17:14

Cause _____ to revere your name. Be her sun of righteousness, rising in her life with healing in its rays.

MALACHI 4:2

Bring health and healing to _____. Let him enjoy abundant peace and security.   JEREMIAH 33:6

Have compassion on _____ and heal her.

MATTHEW 14:14

Let _____ take refuge in you and be glad; let him sing for joy. Spread your protection over _____, that he may rejoice in you. PSALM 5:11

Look upon _____ and heal her. Guide her and comfort her, creating praise on her lips. Give her peace wherever she goes. ISAIAH 57:18–19

CHAPTER 13

Praying for Mental and Emotional Health

I waited patiently for the LORD;
he turned to me and heard my cry.
He lifted me out of the slimy pit,
out of the mud and mire;
He set my feet on a rock
and gave me a firm place to stand.
He put a new song in my mouth,
a hymn of praise to our God.

PSALM 40:1–3

Ginny could hardly wait to see her son. Walker had finished his sophomore year at college and accepted a summer internship with an investment firm in New York City. Ginny had rallied the whole family—her husband, Jim, plus Walker's two younger sisters, Molly and Maggie—to make the trek to the Big Apple for a weekend at the end of the summer. They had only been at their hotel for ten minutes when Walker rapped on the door. Twelve-year-old Maggie flung it open—and gasped.

"Who are you, and what have you done with my brother?"

Walker was, indeed, hard to recognize. His hair was long and unkempt; he had grown a beard; and it was clear that he had lost a lot of weight. At six foot two, Walker had left for college carrying 185 pounds; now it looked like he weighed about 120.

Ginny had known her son was dropping weight, and the last time she'd seen him, his normally clean-shaven face and preppy haircut had been replaced by more of what she called "the grunge look," but none of that had concerned her. College kids went through all sorts of changes, didn't they? Some gained weight and some lost it, and everybody tweaked their outfits and their hairstyles. Walker was still making the straight A's he had earned in high school; Ginny and Jim were confident that their high-achieving son was just going through some sort of phase.

Now, though, she wasn't so sure. Surrounded by his family, Walker began talking, rapid-fire, about his plans for the future. "I am going to lead a revival in this city," he said, smiling broadly.

"What about your internship?" Jim asked. "How did that go?"

"God told me I didn't need to finish that," Walker replied. "Everyone here is so into making money and getting rich; I'm not. I'm more into helping people. I gave all my money away."

Jim and Ginny exchanged a look. They had always taught their children to be generous—Ginny had even texted Walker a Bible verse about being willing to share with those in need—but this seemed a little extreme. She was glad they had planned to tour the city and then head home with Walker for a couple of weeks before he was due to go back to college. She didn't want to leave him alone.

At home, though, things got worse. Walker's affable personality took on a somber, dangerous-sounding tone. "There is darkness in this house," he declared. "And there is darkness in you, Mom."

Ginny and Jim realized that the situation was spiraling out of control. They needed to get help, and fast. They called a doctor friend who confirmed that they should take Walker to the hospital, even though it was the middle of the night. "I was terrified," Ginny told me. "I didn't want to do that. No parent wants to be in the Take Your Child to the Hospital club. But in a way, I was also relieved."

That evening began a years-long journey that is still unfolding. Doctors diagnosed Walker with bipolar disorder, a mental illness often characterized by things like rapid mood changes, grandiose plans and ideas, impulsive overspending or generosity, loud or fast talking, and other high-energy behaviors that can last for hours or days.[1]

Walker accepted the diagnosis and agreed to take medication. But that was no easy fix. He was a smart and quick-thinking student who was used to excelling at pretty much every endeavor—from captaining his high school lacrosse team to

---

1. See Grant Mullen, MD, *Emotionally Free: A Prescription for Healing Body, Soul, and Spirit*, 2nd ed. (Mustang, OK: Tate, 2013), 100–101.

giving the sermon on Youth Sunday at church—and he found himself frustrated as he worked to adjust to the medicine's side effects. "It was like putzin' along in a Pinto," Ginny confided, "when he was used to driving a race car. It was hard for him to get any mental traction."

Unable to return to college, Walker got a job making sandwiches at a local deli frequented by Ginny's neighbors and friends. "Why isn't Walker back at school this semester?" people wanted to know.

Depending on who was asking, Ginny offered "the short story, the medium story, or the long story"—but in every case, she was honest about what their family was facing. "Walker is working through some mental health issues," she told people. "We're getting help, and we're hopeful for the future."

"You are so brave," one woman said. "I don't know if I could be so open about a mental or emotional illness in my family."

"I don't feel brave at all," Ginny replied. "I mean, people can *tell* that something is going on just by looking at Walker. I don't want to stay in the dark; I want to bring our situation into the light. We have to get rid of the shame and the stigma that surround mental illness. People need to be able to support each other—we need our praying friends, now more than ever."

For Ginny, hope and support came in many forms, including through a book called *Emotionally Free*. The author, Grant Mullen, is a medical doctor who set out to demystify the labels and treatment options for what he calls "emotional bondage."

In the Christian community, especially, Mullen says, there can sometimes be an "unspoken message that emotional illness [is] a sign of spiritual and emotional weakness and that strong Christians really shouldn't suffer from these conditions" but should be able to "get out of it themselves."[2]

===== *Prayer Principle* =====

When you pray your child through a mental or emotional illness, don't let shame or fear keep you from enlisting trusted prayer partners to help carry your burden.

Nothing, Mullen maintains, could be further from the truth. His vision for emotional health and wholeness resembles a three-legged stool: The physical part of a person, the behavioral part (the mind, will, and emotions), and the spiritual part. With brain disorders such as depression, anxiety, schizophrenia, bipolar disorder, and attention deficit disorder, addressing the physical causes with medication (treating "blurred thinking" the way you would treat "blurred vision," for instance) can help restore proper brain chemistry. But medicine alone, Mullen says, is not the answer; he endorses the value of emotional counseling, as well as the need for stepping into the spiritual dimension of healing through prayer.

---

2. Ibid., 31.

======= *Prayer Principle* =======

God is in the business of transformation, and he has promised
to renew us—body, mind, and spirit—day by day.[3]

For Ginny, Mullen's threefold approach made sense. After
receiving a diagnosis and beginning medical treatment, she and
Jim joined a bipolar support group at their church. Together with
Walker, they drew strength from professional counselors who
emphasized the importance of maintaining structure (things like
working in the deli) as part of the journey to emotional freedom.
And they confided their deepest concerns to a trusted group
of praying friends who fought the battle on the spiritual front.

Even with this support, though, Ginny and Jim could not
help but grow weary. They found themselves tempted to doubt
God's goodness or his power to heal, wondering if maybe he loved
other people, but not their family. To combat these thoughts
(which they recognized as lies), they made a deliberate (and sometimes difficult) choice to focus on the truth. "Every day," Ginny
said, "we would say the same thing, and we'd say it out loud: *God
is good. He is powerful. And he loves me.*"

This emphasis on God's goodness and power gave rise to
hope—a hope that grew as Ginny and Jim began to see positive
changes in their son. *Could he*, they wondered, *return to college?*

---

3. 2 Corinthians 4:16; Romans 12:2; Psalm 51:10.

That was certainly what they all wanted, and with the blessing of Walker's medical team, they agreed to give it a go. He made his way through the next year and a half, but then sank into a deep depression, becoming catatonic and losing even more weight. For Ginny, the setback was devastating. "We thought he was doing so well, and that he was stable. The fact that we were wrong—and that we had to bring him home and hospitalize him again, and that he was actually *worse*—created a fear in me of what might happen next."

One of Walker's doctors added fuel to these fears. "His cognition will likely never return," the man warned. "He will never go back to college."

Beaten and broken—and yet unwilling to give up hope—Ginny and Jim made the difficult decision to move Walker to a long-term therapeutic community that offered more aggressive treatment options. After nearly two months, he seemed much improved. Still, though, he rarely spoke, and they knew more had to be done. Ginny found herself crying out to God, searching the Scriptures for some way to cope with both her present reality and her fears for the future—worries that Walker might never get better, that he would try to take his own life, or that (given the genetic links Ginny knew were associated with mental illness) one of her daughters would become afflicted.

Habakkuk 3:17–19 became Ginny's spiritual touchstone, as she exchanged the prophet's desperate circumstances for her own worst nightmares and turned his words into her own resolute prayer:

> *Though Walker never gets better and sits in the house for*
> *the rest of his life, though he threatens to commit suicide and*
> *even succeeds in killing himself, though he gets better for a*
> *little while and then gets worse again and we live on a roller*
> *coaster for the rest of our lives, though more of our children*
> *and grandchildren develop mental health issues, YET I*
> *will rejoice in the Lord; I will be joyful in God my Savior.*
> *The Sovereign Lord is my strength; he makes my feet like*
> *the feet of the deer; he enables me to tread on the heights.*

Even as she vowed to choose joy—whether or not Walker's condition improved—Ginny continued to pray for his healing. She had been raised in a traditional church (one where miracles and supernatural displays were not often discussed), but when she heard about a conference offered through Christian Healing Ministries, she decided to attend.[4] She figured she could hang out in the back and just watch. And when the leader invited people to come forward for prayer, she stayed seated—until she sensed God speaking to her heart. "I made you," he said, "and I know you. If you want to sit in the back of the room with your arms crossed, that's okay. I can still bless you."

Disarmed by God's love, Ginny made her way to the front. One of the prayer leaders asked God to reveal any areas of unforgiveness that might be getting in the way of healing.

---

4. For more information about Christian Healing Ministries, visit www .christianhealingmin.org.

Immediately, Ginny had a strong impression that God wanted
her to forgive *herself*. That seemed odd, at first, until a torrent of
memories—coupled with ugly accusations—flooded her mind:

- Her own family had a genetic history of mental illness;
  Walker's problem was probably all her fault.
- Walker was her oldest child; no wonder she had made
  so many mistakes!
- And what about that young woman she met at church,
  the one who had looked at her family and then
  unwittingly let loose a dagger: "You seem like such a
  good mom. How could this happen?" Clearly, people
  assumed Ginny had done something wrong—and
  maybe they were right.

As Ginny turned these thoughts over in her head, they were
replaced with a mental picture. She saw herself hanging on a
giant meat hook and heard the Lord whispering to her spirit:
*You need to forgive yourself. You have to let yourself off the hook
so that I can go to work.*

Not sure how to proceed, Ginny simply surrendered her will
and told God she had forgiven herself. And then, for good measure, she mentally forgave Walker for the pain he had unwillingly
caused, as well as her parents for any part they may have played
in contributing to a genetic pattern or saddling her with the
responsibility to "fix" things.

"I literally felt my brain tingle," Ginny said, "and it was like my fears simply vanished. The meat hook was gone, and I felt free." Ginny had no idea what had happened in the spiritual realm, but she had the distinct sense that something had given way. The path to healing was open.

=========== *Prayer Principle* ===========

An unforgiving spirit can hinder your prayers.
Ask God to search your heart—and be ready to extend
grace (even to yourself) and receive God's love.

Sure enough, Walker began to change. Spring was in the air, and as the trees and flowers blossomed, so did he—talking and laughing and slowly regaining his confidence and his joy. He got a job with a construction company, doing the most menial labor but flourishing under the structure and his newfound sense of responsibility and purpose.

Eventually, Walker went back to college, earning not just his BA but also, two years later, a master's degree. None of that was easy—it was like "running a marathon on crutches," Ginny says—and it required some major adjustments on Walker's part (letting go of the need to make good grades, for example, and being willing to allow other people to hold him accountable and help track his moods rather than relying on his own intelligence and ability). Still, though, Ginny looks back on all that they have been through—and all that the future holds—and maintains that their family has been blessed.

"We were living the dream, raising a son who succeeded at everything. I didn't know it then, but it was like we had set up two idols on our mantel: appearance and achievement. Those idols got smashed, along with our pride—which, ultimately, opened the door to real freedom and emotional security.

"I know it might not look this way," she continues, "but ours is a story of great hope. Doctors said it would never work—and I understand the need to balance reality with faith—but something always happens when we pray."

Poised for Prayer

Every year, about 42.5 million American adults (or about one in five of us) suffer from some form of mental illness, enduring conditions such as depression, bipolar disorder, or schizophrenia. Some estimates put that number even higher, saying the prevalence of mental illness among adults is closer to 25 or 30 percent.[5] Experts agree that many of these disorders begin in adolescence but are often not detected due to the public perception that it is normal for teens to be emotionally unstable—and even once the symptoms have been present for years, the problem is often overlooked. Among adults

---

5. Victoria Bekiempis, "Nearly 1 in 5 Americans Suffers from Mental Illness Each Year," *Newsweek*, February 28, 2014, www.newsweek.com/nearly-1-5-americans -suffer-mental-illness-each-year-230608 (accessed April 11, 2017).

with "severe" mental illness (things like schizophrenia or bipolar disorder), the 2012 National Survey on Drug Use and Health reported that 40 percent received no treatment at all.

Here's how one reporter summed up the problem: "The mentally ill who have nowhere to go and find little sympathy from those around them often land hard in emergency rooms, county jails and city streets. The lucky ones find homes with family. The unlucky ones show up in the morgue."[6]

I had to read that paragraph twice. The "lucky ones" wind up with family? I guess, considering the alternative, that's a true statement . . . but honestly, I couldn't see anything "lucky" about mental illness, no matter where a person wound up.

But then I thought back to Ginny's words about how God had worked in their family and how he was (and still is) using their story to bring comfort, hope, and healing to others. Ginny would be the first to say that she would not wish mental illness on anyone, but she would also tell you that God has brought great good from something so broken and bad.

Listening to her talk about smashing the idols of achievement, appearance, and pride, I thought of the story in Mark 14, the one where Jesus knows he is about to go to the cross and where Mary, the sister of Lazarus, brings an alabaster jar of expensive perfume and breaks it, pouring the precious liquid on

---

6. Liz Szabo, "Cost of Not Caring: Nowhere to Go," *USA Today*, May 12, 2014, www.usatoday.com/story/news/nation/2014/05/12/mental-health-system-crisis/7746535 (accessed April 11, 2017).

Jesus' head. I'm no theologian, but I think at least three things happened when the jar broke.

First, the home was filled with fragrance. Mary's gift was costly (the jar was worth about a year's wages), and it showed her deep devotion to Jesus. She loved him, and she didn't care who knew it. In the same way, I believe Ginny and Jim's willingness to be "broken" in front of their community—to share their painful journey, to love their neighbors, and to openly proclaim their hope in Christ—spread the fragrance of God's love and comfort to others who needed to know he was there.

Next, Mary was criticized. The Bible tells us that people got indignant over what she had done; why would she "waste" the perfume when it could have been sold to help care for the poor? Likewise, Ginny and her family have endured criticism (why would they talk about mental illness so openly?) and mis-understanding (as people wondered why they were suffering or speculated about what they had done wrong). And yet nothing about their story was wasted or wrong; instead, God continues to use them to bring light and hope to one of the darkest and most frightening problems of our day.

And finally, Jesus commended Mary, saying that what she had done was "a beautiful thing." Ginny, I think, would under-stand the Lord's words. Not because of anything she has done, but because she knows that, in God's tender hands, good can come out of evil, light can shine out of darkness, and things like brokenness and shame can become pathways to beauty.

Prayers You Can Use

For Yourself

Heavenly Father . . .

When our family suffers, let us not be ashamed. Instead, let us be confident in your ability to guard whatever we entrust to you, including our child's emotional health.

2 TIMOTHY 1:12

Help me believe that I will receive what I ask you for. Equip me to forgive people (including myself), even as you forgive me.

MARK 11:24–25

Thank you for taking what is meant for harm and using it for good. Let us not be afraid but trust you to provide for our children.

GENESIS 50:20–21

For Your Children

Heavenly Father . . .

May _____ be still and know that you are God.

PSALM 46:10

Cause _____ to revere your name, and may the sun of righteousness rise in his life, with healing in its rays.

MALACHI 4:2

Lead _____ by ways she has not known; guide her along the unfamiliar [treatment] paths. Turn her darkness into light, and make the rough places smooth. Do not forsake her.

ISAIAH 42:16

Remind _____ that you are with him, that you are mighty, and that you take great delight in him. Quiet _____ by your love, and rejoice over him with singing.

ZEPHANIAH 3:17 NIV, ESV

Fight this battle for _____; let her know she only needs to be still.

EXODUS 14:14

Mark _____'s life with love, joy, peace, forbearance, kindness, goodness, faithfulness, gentleness, and self-control.

GALATIANS 5:22–23

May _____'s light break forth like the dawn and his recovery speedily spring forth. May righteousness go before _____, and may your glory, Lord, be his rear guard.

ISAIAH 58:8

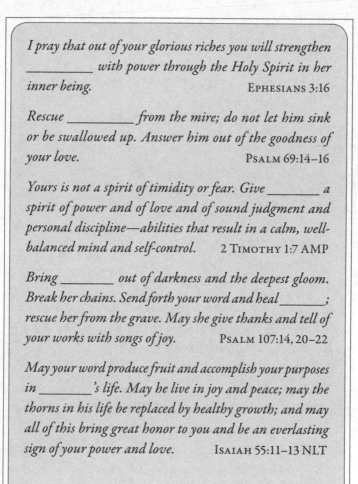

I pray that out of your glorious riches you will strengthen _____ with power through the Holy Spirit in her inner being.   Ephesians 3:16

Rescue _____ from the mire; do not let him sink or be swallowed up. Answer him out of the goodness of your love.   Psalm 69:14–16

Yours is not a spirit of timidity or fear. Give _____ a spirit of power and of love and of sound judgment and personal discipline—abilities that result in a calm, well-balanced mind and self-control.   2 Timothy 1:7 AMP

Bring _____ out of darkness and the deepest gloom. Break her chains. Send forth your word and heal _____; rescue her from the grave. May she give thanks and tell of your works with songs of joy.   Psalm 107:14, 20–22

May your word produce fruit and accomplish your purposes in _____'s life. May he live in joy and peace; may the thorns in his life be replaced by healthy growth; and may all of this bring great honor to you and be an everlasting sign of your power and love.   Isaiah 55:11–13 NLT

CHAPTER 14

Praying for Protection from Harm

The angel of the LORD encamps
around those who fear him.

PSALM 34:7

Ping.

Laura awoke to the beep and reached for the phone on her nightstand, checking the clock as she did so: 5:30 a.m. Who would text her so early in the morning?

Is Steve all right?

Rubbing the sleep from her eyes, Laura reread her friend's text. What did she mean, *Is Steve all right?* Had there been some sort of accident or—it seemed impossible—an attack?

A quick Google search confirmed Laura's fears. Two helicopters had collided off the coast of Hawaii—choppers from K-Bay, the Marine Corps base in Kaneohe, Hawaii. Early reports indicated that twelve Marines were missing, and based on eyewitness accounts of a "big fireball" in the night, hopes for finding any survivors were dim.

Laura's heart froze. Steve was stationed at Kaneohe, and he had been scheduled to fly that night. Laura's son was a Navy pilot, not Marine Corps, but how easy it would be for reporters to mix up a detail like that, given that helicopters from both branches flew from the same base.

Laura needed more information. Even if the media was right, and the missing service members were Marines and not a Navy crew, there was a reasonable chance that they were friends of Steve's. Helo pilots and their crews were a tight-knit bunch. Tragedies involving helicopters during training missions had occurred in unprecedented numbers during the last eighteen months or so, and this wouldn't be the first time Steve had lost someone he knew.

And, Laura realized, even if the crash victims *were* Marines and not Navy guys, twelve brave souls had more than likely lost their lives—and twelve mothers' hearts would be broken. The loss of a child is every parent's worst nightmare; it's no wonder that all parents worry about their children's physical well-being even years after they've left home. And perhaps no one grapples with this fear more than military parents, whose children willingly put themselves in harm's way as part of their job.

Laura's mind flashed back to Steve's graduation day in Annapolis. He had looked tall and handsome standing in the

May sunshine, and his expression said what Laura had told herself for years: *he was made for this.*

As a young boy, Steve and his brother Peter would stage epic battles with their babysitter, Tom. Laura would often return to find one of the boys crouched defensively behind the sofa (the "rampart," Tom had called it), while the other made an advance by scaling a chair. Sometimes a wrestling match was taking place, and Laura would walk in on a tangle of legs, elbows, and laughter. None of the testosterone-fueled roughhousing had fazed Tom; on the contrary, he encouraged the boys to think and act strategically, to sharpen their minds as well as their bodies.

Laura was not surprised when Tom grew up and accepted an appointment to the US Naval Academy. By then, he had become a dear family friend, and whenever he came home, the one-time babysitter would entertain the boys with stories of endless drills and inspections, along with tales of the grueling physical and academic challenges that marked the life of a midshipman. It was, Laura knew, a grim but fairly realistic picture.

"Can't you spruce it up a bit?" she had teased. "Peter and Steve are going to be applying to college themselves before long, and I don't want them to think that every school is *that* bad."

Rather than discourage the boys, though, Tom's stories worked as a magnet. Steve, in particular, was captivated by the ideals of service and sacrifice, as well as by a desire to test his own limits. Peter went off to college on a track scholarship, but

Steve set his sights on the Naval Academy, and he was thrilled when he received his own appointment.

Laura remembered her chest tightening when the offer came, encased in a stiff binder with a gold seal and a presidential signature. She figured the packaging was meant to impress (it had), but it also seemed to carry a warning: *This. Is. Serious.* She had wanted to protest, to encourage Steve to attend the nearby state university and major in something safe, like English or art history. But she realized that it was one thing for a parent to give advice and quite another to stand in the way of what God might be doing.

"I can't bear the thought of Steve being forty-five years old and having to tell somebody that he had really wanted to go to the Naval Academy," she confided to her husband, Mac, "but that he hadn't gone because his mom wasn't comfortable with that decision."

"Yeah," Mac agreed, "and Steve definitely sees this as a calling and not just a career path. He sees it as a great fit."

"Believe me, I know," Laura said. "Moms know better than anybody how their children are wired. Given Steve's interests and passions, this whole thing makes perfect sense.

Prayer Principle

If God calls your child to a place or a job that scares you, slip your hand into your heavenly Father's and pray, trusting him to guard what you give him.

"But," she said with a sigh, "that doesn't mean I like it."

Four years later, at Steve's commissioning ceremony, Laura felt those old familiar fears wrapping themselves around her heart. Her son had chosen to become a helicopter pilot. Helicoptering (if that was even a word) required teamwork and fostered a strong sense of camaraderie, which appealed to Steve, and the position would allow him to be integral to a variety of missions. Those were the pluses. On the minus side, flying choppers would significantly increase his risk factor in a world already marked by danger. Unlike military jets, helicopters did not come with an "Eject" button.

Laura had slipped her hand through Mac's arm as they watched their son move off to join the other midshipmen, their white hats dazzling in the sunlight. "I would be so proud of any young man who chose this path," she whispered.

"And," she continued after a beat, "I would be so thrilled if it was anybody else's son."

Those words—*anybody else's son*—came flooding back to Laura's mind as she scrambled to get more information about the chopper accident. Twelve young men were missing. It had been nearly two hours since Laura had received her friend's text, and she had been unable to contact her son. Plenty of people had talked to him before he took off with his crew, but no one could confirm that he had landed.

Looking up from her phone, Laura's eyes fell on a cross-stitched sampler that her mother had made for Steve before he was born. She had asked for Laura's input on the piece, and without hesitation, Laura had said, "Psalm 91:11. Put that on there, Mom."

For he will command his angels concerning you to guard you in all your ways.

How many times over the course of Steve's life had Laura prayed that verse? She had lost count. It had certainly been an appropriate petition throughout Steve's high school career, when varsity football and wrestling, as well as things like teenaged driving and parties, meant that virtually every day brought a fresh opportunity for disaster. And Steve *had* landed in the emergency room several times with sports-related injuries, one of which resulted in internal bleeding that nearly took his life. The fact that he had survived that ordeal was, to Laura, proof that God answered prayer.

And the need for angelic protection was not just physical. Laura regularly prayed Psalm 91 over Steve's emotions and his mind, knowing that as he pursued his military career, he would be exposed to everything from pornography to partying to loss of life. Steve was a big guy, but he had a tender heart, and Laura desperately wanted God to guard that for him.

=========== *Prayer Principle* ===========

Asking God to put his angels in charge of your child's safety encompasses more than just physical protection. We can trust him to stand guard over their hearts and minds too.

Now, though, her chief concern was for his physical safety. Her phone buzzed, and she looked down to find a text from one of Steve's friends. Steve had returned from his training flight in the early hours of the morning. He and his crew were safe, but they, like all of America, grieved for the ones who had been lost.

Laura dropped to her knees, relieved as well as heartbroken. She asked God to strengthen and comfort the other mothers who—like her—had released their sons and daughters to follow their dreams, knowing it could one day cost them their lives. The words of Isaiah 40:11, so familiar when her boys were young, flooded her heart: "He tends his flock like a shepherd: He gathers the lambs in his arms and carries them close to his heart; he gently leads those that have young."

Sometimes, she knew, God needed to carry the children. And sometimes he needed to carry their moms.

Poised for Prayer

When Laura told me her story, I asked whether she had ever heard Psalm 91 referred to as the "Soldier's Psalm." She hadn't, and so I told her the unconfirmed report I had heard.

During World War I, the 91st Infantry Brigade of the US Expeditionary Army had a commander who was a devout Christian. As they prepared to enter combat in Europe, the commander gave each man a copy of Psalm 91. The troops are said to have recited the psalm daily, and despite fighting in three of the war's bloodiest battles, the 91st Brigade did not suffer even one combat-related casualty.

Laura was amazed.

"When my mom asked me what I wanted her to sew on Steve's sampler," she said, "I just knew it was supposed to be Psalm 91:11. Don't ask me why; all I can figure is that it's somehow related to Jeremiah 1:5, where God says, 'Before I formed you in the womb I knew you.' God knew who Steve would be and what he would do, and so he gave me Psalm 91 to pray for his life."

I don't know about you, but I find those words from Jeremiah hugely encouraging. God knows our kids and has plans for them, even before they are born. Taken together with a verse like Job 42:2 (which says that no plan of God's can be thwarted), the knowledge that God is "on it" in our kids' lives—and that he has been, since forever—gives us permission to stop holding our breath. These promises give us a reason to trust God and relax.

I have known Laura for more than twenty years, and I can't point to many friends whose faith has been tested (and proved genuine) as much as hers has. She has never wavered—and yet, even though she is confident in God's goodness and she fully believes in his power, she would readily admit that trusting God when your child is up against a clear and present danger is much easier said than done. And there are plenty of days when sadness creeps in: "I knew I would miss Steve on Thanksgiving and Christmas," she jokes, "but until now, I didn't realize how much you could miss your child on Columbus Day!"

Laura is keenly aware of the role that fear can play in her parenting—and in her prayers. "This is a world I don't understand and I didn't sign up for," she says. "I feel more inept and inadequate than I ever thought possible. I cannot, on my own, support my son graciously, gratefully, and from a position of strength.

"And so I pray for myself. My main prayer comes from 2 Corinthians 12:9, which reminds me that God's grace is sufficient, even in the face of my fear, and that his power is made perfect in my abundant weakness."

=== *Prayer Principle* ===

When you feel too frightened or overwhelmed to pray for your child's safety, remember that God's power is made perfect in your weakness.

Regardless of whether or not our children serve in the military, they will all face danger. Maybe it will be in a demanding work environment, or maybe their travels will take them to places where disease, crime, and even terrorism are very real threats. Even if it's just the fact that your daughter lives next to a strip club and takes the New York City subway home alone at night, we will all find ourselves praying at some point for our children's protection. We'll need to fight for their physical safety, their emotional well-being, and their spiritual resilience. And there will be times when, like Laura, we will feel weak, inept, or inadequate. Things like fear and worry will work to paralyze or cripple us. Things like deception and discouragement will try to worm their way in, telling us we are not up to the job or that the problem they face is too big. But don't give ground. Don't cede that territory.

Instead, map out your own battle strategy. Depend on God's all-sufficient grace. And put on your God-given armor: The belt of truth to stabilize you in the face of lies and deception. The breastplate of righteousness, so that your behavior lines up with your identity in Christ. Shoes that will anchor you in God's peace and allow you to move forward as you fight. The shield of faith to inspire you to action. The helmet of salvation to cover your mind and guard your identity in Christ.[1]

And take up your sword—which is the Word of God—and be ready to use it.

---

1. This is the armor Paul describes in Ephesians 6:10–19. For more on this battle gear and how it can impact your prayer life, see Priscilla Shirer's *The Armor of God* study (Nashville: Lifeway, 2015).

Prayers You Can Use

For Yourself

Heavenly Father . . .

When I am weak or frightened, help me remember that your grace is sufficient for me and that your power is made perfect in weakness.   2 CORINTHIANS 12:9

I know you will carry my child close to your heart. Be my shepherd too, and lead me as I pray for him.   ISAIAH 40:11

Help me not to be anxious about anything, but in every situation, by prayer and petition, let me present my requests to you. And may your peace, which passes all understanding, guard my heart and mind in Christ Jesus.

PHILIPPIANS 4:6–7

For Your Children

Heavenly Father . . .

May your faithfulness be _____'s shield and rampart. Do not let her fear the terror of night or the arrow that flies by day.   PSALM 91:4–5

Let no harm befall _____. Command your angels concerning _____ to guard him in all his ways [body, mind, and spirit]. Psalm 91:10–11

Equip _____ to be on her guard, to stand firm in the faith, to be courageous, and to be strong. 1 Corinthians 16:13

When _____ passes through deep waters or fiery trials, be with him. Don't let him be swept away or get burned. Isaiah 43:2

Spread your protection over _____, and let her rejoice in you. Surround her with favor as with a shield. Psalm 5:12

Keep _____ from all harm. Watch over his life, now and forever. Psalm 121:7–8

Give _____ victory and be her shield. Guard her course and protect her way. Proverbs 2:7–8

Bless _____ and expand his territory. Be with him in all he does and keep him from trouble and pain. 1 Chronicles 4:10

Do not let _____ give in to fear or discouragement. Be with her. Strengthen her, help her, and hold her up with your victorious hand.   ISAIAH 41:10 NLT

Hold fast to _____, and help him to hold fast to you. Fight for him, Lord, and let him be very careful to love you.   JOSHUA 23:8, 10

May _____ consider it pure joy when she faces trials, knowing that these tests of faith develop perseverance and that perseverance will make her mature and complete, not lacking anything.   JAMES 1:2–4

Lead _____ not into temptation, but deliver him from evil.   MATTHEW 6:13

CHAPTER 15

Praying through a Job Loss or Financial Difficulty

When I said, "My foot is slipping,"
your unfailing love, LORD, supported me.
When anxiety was great within me,
your consolation brought me joy.

PSALM 94:18–19

When Robbie and I had been married for about eight years, I got a job writing books for Ron Blue, a financial guru who ran a nationally known wealth management company. I'll never forget coming home from work one day and telling Robbie that I had learned the secret to financial freedom.

"What is it?" he eagerly asked.

"It's to spend less than you earn," I crowed, "and do that over a long period of time!"

Robbie rolled his eyes. He had heard that one before. We both had actually (although in my case, it needed repeating). Back when we'd gotten engaged, my father had sent us to a

money management seminar taught by another big-time financial brainiac, Larry Burkett. All my engaged friends were getting
china and crystal from their parents, but Dad figured a better
investment in our marital happiness was to get us an education
about things like saving money, avoiding debt, and tithing.

We were twenty-one years old. At the time, I would have
rather had the wine glasses. Or even a Crock-Pot. But now,
thirty-plus years and several job changes, home purchases, and
stock-market swings later, I bless my father for his foresight. The
seminar didn't keep Robbie and me from making some stupid
financial decisions, but it got us on the same page in terms of
how we would manage our meager newlywed assets, and when
the whoopsies happened, having a biblically based financial game
plan kept us pointed in the right direction.

=== *Prayer Principle* ===

The Bible has a lot to say about money. Ask God to
help your children learn to manage it wisely.

I thought about my dad when I interviewed Chip and Eloise
for this chapter. They didn't send their three children to any
classes or seminars, but they raised them using principles outlined in Scripture, even giving the girls mason jars marked "Save,"
"Spend," and "Give," so that when they got their allowance or
earned babysitting money, they could allocate their resources

wisely. And when their oldest daughter, Claire, grew up and got a job leasing commercial real estate, Chip and Eloise thanked God for what they saw as his blessing and favor. Many of their friends had adult children still living at home; they were grateful that Claire could afford her own apartment, that she knew how to handle her paycheck, and that she seemed to be thriving.

Two years later, though, Claire lost her job. "She's a smart gal, and she loved the financial part of the real estate business," Eloise told me. "But she didn't like the sales aspect of her job. We probably should have seen that coming; she's a numbers person, not a schmoozer."

"A schmoozer!" I laughed. "Who wants to be a schmoozer?"

"You know what I mean. In sales, you have to connect with people and take them to lunch and care about their lives and their business needs—or at least pretend to. That's not who Claire is. She would much rather have lunch at her desk with a bunch of spreadsheets."

Maybe it was her innately conservative nature or maybe it was the mason-jar training, but Claire had managed to accumulate a few months' worth of living expenses in her savings account, and she had been careful to pay off her credit cards every month. She did, however, have a car payment, and without a salary, she knew she wouldn't be able to make rent for very long. She asked Chip and Eloise if she could move back home until she found another job, and they agreed.

"I think Claire really struggled with that," Eloise confided.

"She felt like she had failed, and when the company let her go, she felt the sting of rejection. She couldn't see all the ways God had blessed her, giving her an ability to grasp financial concepts and work with numbers. All she could see was where she had fallen short."

Knowing that their daughter was hurting, but not wanting to overwhelm her with a bunch of unsolicited suggestions or even comforting words, Chip and Eloise were careful not to offer too much in the way of advice. Instead, they took their concerns to God and asked him to bring peace to their daughter's heart.

"Jesus certainly knew what it was like to be rejected," Chip said. "Learning to handle that is, I think, part of growing up. We asked God to use this difficult season to teach Claire about his unconditional love and acceptance, and to turn her anxiety into joy."[1]

Prayer Principle

When we pray our kids through loss or rejection, it helps to remember that Jesus knows exactly how they feel.

In addition to asking God to let Claire know how much she was loved, Chip and Eloise committed to praying daily that she would find a new job, one that would make use of her talents and

1. This is a prayer grounded in Psalm 94:17–18.

skills. "We prayed verses like Psalm 90:17," Eloise said, "asking God to establish the work of Claire's hands and make her efforts successful."

Within a few months, Claire was hired as a project manager for one of the construction companies she had dealt with during her leasing career. Keeping track of supplies, expenses, and deadlines suited her perfectly, and Chip and Eloise again found themselves thanking God for his provision. "It was as though he had created Claire specifically for this job," Eloise marveled. "It was the perfect use of her skills, talents, and interests."

=== *Prayer Principle* ===

God knows how our children are formed, and what they do with their lives matters to him.[2]

Five years later, Chip and Eloise had even more reason to be grateful. Claire had met and married Landon, a terrific young man. They were blessed with a son (Chip and Eloise's first grandchild), and now Claire was expecting another baby. She was still working part-time, and having saved nearly enough money for a down payment, the couple looked forward to buying a home. They spent almost every weekend looking at neighborhoods that offered things like good schools, sidewalks, and parks.

---

2. Psalm 139:13–14; Ephesians 2:10.

And then they got the "can't miss" stock market tip.

"Landon called to ask my advice," Chip recalled. "I don't know that much about the market, but the way he described this investment—which he'd heard about from a college friend who'd become a stockbroker—sounded too good to be true. I told him not to do it. But he and Claire had invested before on this same friend's advice, and I guess they really trusted him."

Claire and Landon took the money they had set aside for their house and gave it to their college friend. Almost before they knew what was happening, their savings had shrunk by half. Claire felt physically ill over the loss—and Eloise told me that she didn't handle it any better.

"I was honestly so frustrated," she said. "Why would Claire and Landon ask for our advice if they weren't going to take it? All I could think about was the verse that says to honor your father and your mother, so that it will go well with you.[3] If only they had listened to Chip, they wouldn't have lost all that money!"

Chip's response was more measured. "I felt bad for the kids," he said, "but again, it was part of growing up. They still had their jobs; they still had each other; and they still had a fine place to rent. All this meant was that it was going to take them a little longer to reach their goal. God wasn't going to abandon them.

"And who knows?" he smiled. "Maybe next time they'll take an old man's advice."

---

3. Deuteronomy 5:16; Ephesians 6:2–3.

Our kids, of course, won't always want to take our advice (and there will be plenty of times when we aren't sure what we'd tell them, even if they *would* listen). But if your kids are open to it, and you want to do like my dad did and bless them with some practical help on things like making a budget, getting out of debt, finding a new career, or setting goals for the future, there are all sorts of resources that can help. Ron Blue's site (www.masteryourmoney.com) offers answers to almost every financial question (purchasing insurance, getting out of debt, buying a home, raising money-smart kids, etc.), along with free videos and other helpful tools; Dave Ramsey's site (www.dave ramsey.com) has links to classes, blogs, and financial advisers; and Crown Financial Ministries (www.crown.org) has help for career transitions, business strategies, and personal financial planning.

Poised for Prayer

Whether troubles come in the form of the pain of unemployment, the loss of money through a bad investment, the challenge of overwhelming debt, or some other financial burden, no parent wants to see an adult child struggle. And when our kids are married, we can find even more reason to worry; all the divorce studies tend to cite one thing as the chief factor in a breakup: money problems.

Ron Blue would say that, in reality, there is no such thing as a money problem.[4] What looks like money trouble is, he says, almost always symptomatic of something else: a distorted view of money, a misunderstanding about how to handle it, or—in the case of married couples—an inability to communicate effectively with each other about finances.

Ron would also tell you that Jesus talked about money more than anything else and that the Bible contains more than 2,300 references to money and possessions.[5] God obviously knew that money—and how to handle it—would be a tricky topic for his people, so he gave us all sorts of pointers:

- Do not wear yourself out to get rich.
- You cannot serve both God and money.
- The one who is unwilling to work shall not eat.
- A generous person will prosper; whoever refreshes others will be refreshed.[6]

With more than two thousand of these money-related verses to pick from, you could probably fill an entire book with prayers on that subject alone. I've pulled a handful of my favorite promises about things like work, money management, financial fear, and generosity; feel free to go hunting for others.

---

4. Ron and Judy Blue, *Money Talks and So Can We* (Grand Rapids: Zondervan, 1999), 11.

5. Ibid., 12.

6. Proverbs 23:4; Matthew 6:24; 2 Thessalonians 3:10; Proverbs 11:25; Proverbs 22:9.

Of course, there is no one-size-fits-all financial strategy, and there is no one-size-fits-all money prayer. As we pray for our adult children, our requests will vary as much as they do. But there is one thing they can all use, one thing we can ask God to provide (even if we have little to offer by way of financial help or an eventual inheritance).

Wisdom.

"By wisdom a house is built," reads Proverbs 24:3–4, "and through understanding it is established; through knowledge its rooms are filled with rare and beautiful treasures."

Ecclesiastes 7:12 adds this: "Wisdom is a shelter as money is a shelter, but the advantage of knowledge is this: Wisdom preserves those who have it."

Money is good, but wisdom is better—particularly given the old maxim that the only thing certain about economic uncertainty is that, sooner or later, it is certain to happen. As we pray for our children's careers, investments, budgeting abilities, and more, let's start by asking God to bless them with wisdom. He doesn't care how many financial mistakes they may have made (or how many we have!); in his capable hands, these things can be woven together to strengthen our shelter against future storms.

Prayers You Can Use

For Yourself

Heavenly Father . . .

When I speak to _____ about things like money and careers, may I speak with wisdom and faithful instruction.
PROVERBS 31:26

Teach me to fear you and to delight in your command so that my children will be mighty, that wealth and riches will be in their houses, and that their righteousness will endure forever.
PSALM 112:1–3

As I consider how or when to help my children financially, help me be sensitive to your timing, knowing there is a time to embrace and a time to refrain, a time to be silent and a time to speak.
ECCLESIASTES 3:5–7

For Your Children

Heavenly Father . . .

May your favor rest on _____; establish the work of his hands.
PSALM 90:17

Do not let _____ wear herself out to get rich; instead, may she realize that the one who gathers money little by little makes it grow.   PROVERBS 23:4; 13:11

When hard times come, remind _____ that you are his refuge, his strength, and his help in trouble—and that he does not need to be afraid.   PSALM 46:1–2

Teach _____ to be content. Don't let her fall into the "get rich" trap or follow foolish desires that will ruin and destroy her.   1 TIMOTHY 6:8–9

Bless all of _____'s skills; be pleased with the work of his hands.   DEUTERONOMY 33:11

Meet all of _____'s needs according to the riches of your glory in Christ Jesus.   PHILIPPIANS 4:19

Show _____ that she doesn't have to worry about what she will eat or drink or wear. Remind her that when she seeks your kingdom first, all of these things will be given to her as well.   MATTHEW 6:31, 33

May _____ honor you with his wealth, so that his barns will be filled to overflowing.   PROVERBS 3:9–10

Make _____ a trustworthy money manager. Show her that whoever can be trusted with little can also be trusted with much.   LUKE 16:10

Remind _____ that wealth and honor come from you. Prompt _____ to be generous, knowing that all he has comes from you.   1 CHRONICLES 29:12, 14

`Help _____ be strong and not give up. Reward her for her work.   2 CHRONICLES 15:7

Let _____ desire wisdom more than money, recognizing that they are both shelters, but that the advantage of knowledge is this: Wisdom preserves those who have it.

                    ECCLESIASTES 7:12

CHAPTER 16

Praying through the Struggles of Infertility

You open your hand
and satisfy the desires of every living thing.
PSALM 145:16

"Though the fig tree does not bud and there are no grapes on the vines, though the olive crop fails and the fields produce no food, though there are no sheep in the pen and no cattle in the stalls, yet I will rejoice in the LORD, I will be joyful in God my Savior."

Cindy reread the words from Habakkuk 3:17–18, words she had underlined in her Bible. The prophet was talking about agriculture, but he might as well have meant grandchildren. Cindy already had three of them—precious babies, born quickly and easily to her daughter, Samantha—but how did that saying go? A mama is only as happy as her saddest child? It was something like that—and right now, Cindy's heart broke for her older daughter, Julia, who had been trying for two years to conceive.

There were no sheep in her pen; her stalls were empty. And Cindy knew that her daughter was hurting.

She read the Habakkuk passage again. "Help us to rejoice, even when we feel empty and things don't make sense," Cindy prayed. "And please give Julia a baby."

Cindy was among the first of my friends to become a grandmother. And in the years since, we've celebrated with a bumper crop of baby showers, as the quivers of the next generation have started collecting their arrows. But there are many nests that remain empty under the pain of miscarriage or barrenness. Having walked the road that no mother or daughter would choose, Julia understands the ache of an unmet longing. At Cindy's suggestion, she agreed to let me share her story.

═══

Julia stared at the pregnancy test, surprised at the sadness that threatened to overtake her soul. The test result was negative—again.

She hadn't expected to feel the disappointment this keenly, but somewhere along the way—maybe it was when she turned thirty—the fun of trying to conceive had become a burden. And if she was really honest with herself, so had all of the baby showers she attended for other people and the meals she cooked for other new moms. Julia wasn't one to let circumstances affect her joy, but her hope was starting to feel crushed under the weight of more than a dozen little discarded sticks, test results that all carried the same discouraging story.

Julia knew people who had longed for something in life—to be married, to get a new job, to start a family—but she had never experienced the pain of a lost expectation or an unmet desire, at least not for very long. She had gone to college, met and married a handsome guy, and landed a job in politics, a field where her natural poise and intellectual curiosity had opened doors to interesting people and exciting opportunities. Julia was at the top of her game—until she wasn't. At age thirty-two, she was ready to become a mother, and for the first time she could remember, nothing was going according to plan.

Tossing the unwanted test result in the trash, Julia reached for her prayer journal. She longed to hear something from God. It didn't matter if he spoke to her about her pregnancy hopes; she just wanted to *hear* him. So many of her friends seemed to have a deeper faith, the kind where they felt like God "told" them things. Julia rarely went a day without Bible reading and prayer, but sometimes it felt like a one-way conversation.

She poured herself a cup of coffee and opened her devotional book, *Streams in the Desert.*

July 1. The devotional began as it always did, with a couple of verses: "My words . . . will come true at their proper time" (Luke 1:20) and "What the Lord has said . . . will be accomplished" (Luke 1:45). Julia turned those words over in her mind, not daring to hope they might apply to her. But then, as she read on, her heart skipped a beat:

The Lord is sure to accomplish those things
    A loving heart has waited long to see;
Those words will be fulfilled to which she clings,
    Because her God has promised faithfully;
And, knowing Him, she ne'er can doubt His Word;
He speaks and it is done. The mighty Lord![1]

Julia hadn't planned to pray about having a baby, but what more was her heart waiting to see if it wasn't a positive result on a pregnancy test? Taking out her purple pen, she bracketed those words and wrote "Baby" in the margin.

And then the strangest thing happened. It was as if God had settled into the chair right beside her, because even though Julia couldn't hear his voice out loud, she had the distinct sense that he was speaking to her. And what he said made her hair stand on end.

"I want you to pray for a baby for one year. I want you to believe there will be a baby."

Could that be right? Julia read the poem again and then looked back at the verses. Taken together, with their emphasis on *timing* and on *belief*, she knew what she had to do. She would pray. And almost as if she could feel the hope kindling unbidden in her heart, she would believe.

She couldn't wait to share what had happened with her

---

1. L. B. Cowman, *Streams in the Desert: 366 Daily Devotional Readings* (Grand Rapids: Zondervan, 1997), 256.

husband, Ryan. He was still in bed, but this was worth waking up for. Julia opened her book and showed him where she'd written the word "Baby." But she hadn't stopped there. She'd also underlined the words quoted from Matthew Henry at the end of the devotional: "We can depend on God to fulfill His promise, even when all the roads leading to it are closed. 'For no matter how many promises God has made, they are "Yes" in Christ. And so through him the "Amen" [so be it] is spoken by us to the glory of God' [2 Cor. 1:20]."

"That's awesome!" Ryan said. "You've been wanting to hear from God, and now you have!"

"But—" Julia stopped, seeing the twinkle in Ryan's eyes. He was as excited about the baby—or at least the *promise* of a baby—as she was. But he had seen the bigger picture. *He knew Julia had been longing, not just for motherhood, but also for a deeper relationship with God*—one where she could pour out her heart and expect him to answer.

"You are so right," Julia said, humbled by the fact that Ryan had seen what she had nearly missed. In answering her heart's cry with the promise of a baby, God had gone above and beyond that request, satisfying her soul with the promise of his presence.

Like Mary after the angelic visit, Julia clung to God's promise. She pondered it in her heart, not telling anyone else what had happened. She knew that more than a year's worth of negative pregnancy tests were no obstacle to God; he had spoken specifically to her, and she resolved to believe him.

====== *Prayer Principle* ======

As you ask God to fulfill your children's deepest longings,
pray that they will be satisfied with the gift of his presence.

After nearly a month, though, she wasn't so sure. Had she really heard God? He had not spoken again; what if she'd just made it all up?

Coffee in hand, Julia grabbed her prayer journal and opened her devotional to July 27: "Test me in this . . . and see if I will not throw open the floodgates of heaven and pour out so much blessing that you will not have room enough for it (Malachi 3:10)."[2]

Test God? That felt strange, wrong even. Julia had grown up knowing better than to try to "test" God. Wasn't it her job to simply believe?

"*Julia.*"

She sensed rather than heard her name. "*I am giving you permission to test me. You didn't come up with that timeline on your own; I gave it to you. Pray for a year.*"

God had spoken again. Taking out her pen once more, Julia put two big stars by the Malachi reference and then wrote out a pledge: "7/27/14. One-year commitment and promise to God." She would pray about her baby for a year and wait to see how God answered.

---

2. Ibid., 288.

Still, though, she didn't tell anyone. Too many friends had gone public with the "good news" that they were trying to get pregnant or that they thought they had conceived, only to face a barrage of questions and expectations. Julia didn't have any news she felt ready to share; all she had was a promise.

And then her mom, one of just a few people who knew about Julia's two-year struggle, broached the subject.

"If I were you," Cindy said gently, "I would want to know. I mean, if there is some sort of problem. I would go to the doctor. You could start with Ryan and just have him get checked . . ."

Cindy let her words hang in the air. She was surprised to see Julia smiling.

"I'm not going to do that, Mom," she said. "I want to get pregnant—you know I do. But I feel like God told me to trust him on this one. He said I'm supposed to pray for one year and that I'm supposed to believe I will have a baby."

Julia was not given to exaggeration, and Cindy couldn't remember ever hearing her daughter say that God had told her anything—at least not anything that specific. But if the Lord had spoken (and Cindy certainly knew he could), she wasn't about to argue.

"He gave me Malachi 3:10," Julia continued, relieved to finally be sharing her story. "It's a verse about testing God and watching him open the floodgates of heaven."

"Wow," Cindy said. "Okay then. I will be praying and trusting God with you."

Cindy had no idea what God had in store, but the fact that God had given Julia a promise (and reinforced it with a Bible verse) was all she needed. She felt an inexplicable peace settle over her heart, a heart that had—just moments before—been anxious for her daughter's happiness.

Prayer Principle

When God gives your children a promise,
come alongside them and believe it.

Julia loved knowing that her mother shared her secret—her promise from God—and that she was praying for its fulfillment. Together, they waited to see what God would do.

A month passed, and then two. Julia's story—the timeline, the testing, the trust—began to feel a little contrived, and when each new pregnancy test came back negative, the darkness advanced. Not normally given to tears, she finally broke down. "I never thought having a baby would mean this much to me," she cried, burying her face in Ryan's chest.

Her sobs grew. "I don't want to be jealous of our friends," she said. "I want to share their joy. I want to visit them in the hospital, to hear their childbirth stories, to bring them presents and food. God has blessed them . . . I want to be happy!"

Julia knew that God's plans didn't always mirror hers. Verses like Isaiah 55:8 ("My thoughts are not your thoughts, neither are your ways my ways") weren't exactly comforting, but they had taught her to keep an open mind, since ultimately God's plans were better. She and Ryan wanted a baby; maybe God wanted them to adopt.

"Pray for a baby for one year."

The Lord's words came back to Julia, along with a new realization. If God was leading them to adopt, maybe "her" baby was being conceived (or even being born) right now and her job was to cover these tender first months in prayer. Julia didn't know. All she knew was that she wanted to be obedient to God.

She wanted to trust him.

And she wanted to be joyful.

None of that was going to be easy—particularly against the backdrop of a calendar filled with baby showers, hospital visits, and meals to cook for an endless parade of new mothers. "You are going to have to help me, Lord," Julia prayed. "I am clinging to you. You are going to have to help me choose joy."

A few nights later, Julia dreamed she was pregnant. She'd resolved not to do any more pregnancy tests—they were too depressing—but the vision had been so real that, when she woke up, she had to find out. It was only 5:00 in the morning, but she did the test and set it aside while she brewed the coffee. It was going to be a long day (another meal for another new mom had to be fixed and delivered), and already she felt tired.

Reaching for her prayer journal, Julia stole a glance at the test. (It was pointless, she knew, but she had to check.)

It was positive.

What? Could she still be dreaming? Julia looked again, and sure enough, the results were unmistakable. She fell to the floor, tears of joy streaming down her face. "Thank you, Lord!" she cried. "Thank you!"

She was in a daze. She knew she had to tell Ryan. First, though, she had to take care of her baby! Julia had been around enough new moms to know that caffeine wasn't good for a child. She dumped her fresh brew into the sink and ran into the bedroom.

Eight months later, Julia and Ryan brought Ryan Jr. home from the hospital. It was July 1, a year to the day from when God had spoken.

Poised for Prayer

I love Julia's story on so many levels. I love how God gave her a promise, and then how Cindy came alongside her to believe it— the way the biblical Elizabeth did when she learned that Mary, her young unmarried relative, was carrying the Son of God.

I love how Julia's husband looked beyond the promise to identify the bigger blessing in God's answer. Julia wanted to hear from God—to sense his active engagement in her life—and she did.

And I love how, in the midst of an almost unimaginable grieving season, Julia pressed into Jesus.

Today, more than one in eight US couples has trouble conceiving or sustaining a pregnancy.[3] I've talked with some of these would-be mothers—women who ache for the blessing of a baby but find themselves cradling a burden instead. For some, the burden is shame ("People look at you and wonder what's wrong with you," one young woman confided); for others, it's a mixture of confusion, disappointment, and a sense of incompleteness or loss. These women know what it's like to have hope deferred. They know what it's like to feel heartsick. And when they read the second part of the Proverbs 13:12 promise, it's like looking through the window at someone else's life:

"Hope deferred makes the heart sick, *but a longing fulfilled is a tree of life.*"

Having lived on both sides of the comma, Julia understands both the pain and the joy in the proverb. But her sense of fulfillment, she says, didn't just come from having a baby; it came, in part, from what she calls "the long road"—a road she never wanted to walk, but one that led her to a deeper knowledge of God.

"It seems easy to say now, since my waiting is over," she said, "but I really am thankful for what this process has taught me. I have a better understanding of what it means to trust God. I am more sensitive to other people during their seasons of longing. And I finally have proof of what I've wanted to know my whole life: God is a God who hears."

---

3. "About Infertility: Medical Conditions," *Resolve.org*, www.resolve.org/about-infertility/medical-conditions (accessed April 11, 2017).

God is a God who hears.

We may think we know what we're asking for, but God hears the cries of our hearts. His love reaches into the deepest recesses of our minds; his understanding penetrates the secret places of our souls. We may want him to give us a material answer—a baby or some other blessing—but he may want to give us more of himself.

Which is hard sometimes. Many of us, if we're honest, would say we want both. Yes, we want our children to know the Provider, but we also want them to enjoy his provision. Is that bad?

No. God invites us to ask him for stuff. "Pray about everything," the Bible says. "Tell God what you need."[4] But when the answer is a long time in coming—when God takes our adult children through a season of waiting—let's not give in to doubt or despair.

Instead, let's come alongside them in their longing, offering comfort and understanding even as we step back and regard the bigger picture: that God can use their unmet desires to grow their faith and even increase their hunger—not just for his blessings, but for his presence. When outcomes are uncertain and the only thing we have to hold on to is God's hand, let's tether our trust to his promises and echo the song that Mary sang: God's mercy extends from generation to generation, and he lifts up the humble and fills the hungry. He satisfies our souls with good things.[5]

---

4. Philippians 4:6 NLT.
5. Paraphrased from Mary's song in Luke 1:46–55.

Prayers You Can Use

For Yourself

Heavenly Father . . .

When everything feels empty and nothing makes sense— when there are no grapes on the vines, no sheep in the pen—help me to rejoice in you and to be joyful because you are my Savior. HABAKKUK 3:17–18

As I consider what to say to my hurting child, equip me to comfort her as you comfort me, and may your comfort overflow into her life. 2 CORINTHIANS 1:3–5

When my heart wants to give in to fear or doubt, help me remember that no purpose of yours can be thwarted.

JOB 42:2

For Your Children

Heavenly Father,

Hear _____ when she cries out to you, for you are compassionate. EXODUS 22:27

Grant _____ a steadfast heart, and keep him in perfect peace as he waits on you. Help him to trust in your timing.
ISAIAH 26:3

You have settled the barren woman in her home as a happy mother of children. Do this for _____, and may she praise you.
PSALM 113:9

May _____'s fountain be blessed; may he rejoice in the wife of his youth.
PROVERBS 5:18

Lift up _____ when she is bowed down; open your hand and satisfy her desire to be a mother.
PSALM 145:14–16

Fulfill _____'s desire to be a father; hear his cry and save him.
PSALM 145:19

You are the Father of compassion. Comfort _____, and may she comfort others who suffer the pain of infertility.
2 CORINTHIANS 1:3–4

Show _____ how to be considerate as he lives with his wife. May he always treat her with respect, knowing that together they are heirs of the gracious gift of life.
1 PETER 3:7

You are the God who gives life to the dead and calls into being things that were not. Create life in _____'s body, and call her "mother."   Romans 4:17

Crown _____ with love and compassion; satisfy his desires with good things, and renew his youth like the eagle's.
Psalm 103:4–5

Be wonderful to _____. Bring rains to their drought-stricken lives. When they go out with heavy hearts, bring them home laughing, with armloads of blessing.
Psalm 126:3–6 MSG

Children are a reward from you, Lord. They are like finely crafted arrows. Bless _____ with a full quiver of them!
Psalm 127:3–5

PART 5

PRAYING
for Your ADULT
CHILD'S *Victory*
over Temptation

CHAPTER 17

Praying for Strength to Resist a Party Culture

Blessed are those who hunger and thirst
for righteousness, for they will be filled.

MATTHEW 5:6

I remember telling my father that I wanted to attend the University of Virginia. The school had recently won top honors in *Playboy* magazine's annual catalog of hot collegiate party spots, and my dad was understandably concerned. Making matters worse (for me) was the fact that one of his best friends—a minister—had sent his son to U.Va., and the fella had gotten into all kinds of mischief. "I wouldn't send my *dog* to that school," the minister had warned, and I thought I was doomed.

Two things, though, worked in my favor. The first was the fact that I knew the minister's son, and he turned out okay. He had graduated and gotten married and had even wound up going to seminary. God clearly had his hand on that boy's life, and I figured he could watch out for me too.

The second thing I had was a working knowledge of Scripture and a willingness to use it (even out of context): "'Where sin abounded,'" I said to my father, quoting the King James Version's rendering of Romans 5:20, "'grace did much more abound.' Come on, Dad. Don't you want me to go to a school where grace *abounds*?"

I won in the end (probably more because U.Va. was the least expensive school on my list than because of the whole sin-and-grace thing). I dove headlong into the social scene, pledging a sorority, dancing the night away at any fraternity house that was having a party, and hanging out in bars where I could order large pitchers of beer and have long conversations about Jesus. Seriously. I figured that most of my sorority sisters and fraternity dates weren't going to show up at church, so if I wanted them to hear the gospel message, I was going to have to take it to where they were.

U.Va., as it turned out, had (and still has) a thriving Christian community, and God blessed me with two very smart, very godly, and very funny roommates. They posted SAT vocabulary words (like *corybantic*, which we used to describe our "frenzied and unrestrained" dance moves) and obscure Bible verses (like Proverbs 23:35, which basically describes a bad hangover) as visible reminders of what *not* to do in the foyer of our apartment, where all of our friends could read them. Between their friendship and God's mercy (and despite my making a boatload of stupid decisions), I graduated, got a job, married Robbie, and never thought much about the college party culture again.

Until my own kids grew up. Dropping Hillary off at college—amid a sea of red Solo cups—I had all sorts of questions. Had the party scene gotten worse? Would she be exposed to a lot of drugs? Sexual pressure? Should I advise her to avoid Greek life? And was the same God who had kept both me and the minister's kid from doing any permanent damage to ourselves or our reputations still on the job?

Pretty much the only answer I was sure about was the last one: God was definitely still on the job. And suddenly, all of his promises about always being with us and with our children seemed more valuable than ever.[1]

=========== *Prayer Principle* ===========

Your adult children may be out of your reach,
but they are never out of God's.

Truth be told, though, I wanted more than a promise that God would be with my girl. I wanted some sort of guarantee that all of those parenting books and "Growing Kids God's Way" classes I had been through would stand Hillary—and her siblings—in good stead, that they wouldn't do the same dumb things I had done, and that when they went off to college or to their careers, they would be like the young Daniel living in

---

1. See, for example, Exodus 33:14; Joshua 1:9; Matthew 28:20; Hebrews 13:5.

Babylon, eating vegetables instead of late-night cheesy bread, drinking water instead of wine, and being "well informed, quick to understand, and qualified to serve."[2]

I wanted that guarantee—that magic formula—but I'm not telling you anything you don't already know when I say that I didn't get it. And after seeing my four children grow up (and talking to dozens of parents about their own kids' experiences), the only thing I know to be true about the party culture and its impact on our adult children is that it is out there—from college bars to corporate boardrooms—and they will be tempted.

Patrick is a self-described Christian raised by parents who went to church every week, said prayers before meals, and read all of James Dobson's parenting books. Fun-loving and gregarious by nature, Patrick quickly made friends in college, and his mom was not at all surprised when he joined one of the most social fraternities on campus. What did surprise her (stun her, actually) was the DUI he got when he offered to drive a crew of guys to some girl's beach house for a party weekend, and the subsequent revelation that he had started smoking pot.

Jamie works for his uncle's roofing company. He had little interest in going to college, and when his uncle offered him a full-time job on one of his crews, he accepted. He had worked construction during his high school summers and knew that a lot of the guys liked to kick back after work; what he wasn't

---

2. See Daniel 1.

prepared for was the pressure he would face to join them. Most of his friends had gone away to school and, not having many other options for his social life, he found himself tagging along when the guys went barhopping. "I didn't worry about Jamie at first," his mom confided, "but he is a people-pleaser, and he goes out almost every night. I just don't want him to get stuck in a rut or to feel like he has to drink to have fun."

For Tom, who works for a Fortune 500 company, the pressure isn't so much from his coworkers as from his higher-ups. Tom has learned that part of making deals involves wining and dining his clients—as well as entertaining them on overnight trips built around hunting, fishing, and drinking. Spouses are not included on the getaways, and as Tom looks at the firm's senior management, he sees a lot of struggling marriages, drinking problems, and divorces. "He knows that's not what he wants his life to look like down the road," Tom's mom told me. "But he's making good money and just got promoted, so I don't think he'll switch jobs anytime soon."

Patrick, Jamie, and Tom. Three very different young men who have at least one thing in common: their parents are praying. None of their mothers object to the fact that their sons like to go out with their friends and coworkers, or even that they drink. What does concern them, they told me, is the subtle way that today's alcohol-fueled social scene opens the door to other, more destructive behaviors and, more importantly, counterfeits the genuine joy and abundant life that can only be found in Jesus.

Today's party culture offers counterfeit joy. Pray
that your kids will want the real thing.

Jamie's mom is asking God to give her son the strength to
stand firm in the face of temptation and to provide him with
some new friends and social opportunities that don't revolve
around drinking. Tom's mother is praying along the same lines,
asking God to give her son discernment as he weighs the allure
of an attractive salary against the potential side effects of the
corporate culture. "I know he feels torn," she says. "I also know
that the enemy wants to destroy Tom's health and his relationships, and even his career. So I'm praying Acts 26:18, that God
would open my son's eyes and turn him from darkness to light,
from the power of Satan to God."

And Patrick's mom is continuing a prayer she has prayed his
whole life. "I've always prayed that if my kids were doing anything wrong, they'd get caught," she told me with a bittersweet
smile.[3] "And they have—the DUI was just one more example
of God's faithfulness in answering that prayer. But as Patrick
turns the corner into adulthood, I'm asking God to lead him to
maturity, to protect him, and to help him turn his back on the
bad stuff and go after good things. We dedicated Patrick to the

---

3. The prayer that our children will be caught in wrongdoing finds its roots in
verses like Numbers 32:23 and Galatians 6:7.

Lord when he was baptized as a baby, and we are counting on God working through that covenant promise to lead him into a life-changing relationship with Christ."

I love how these moms are praying. They know that their sons are like Daniel, up against a Babylonian-style culture where alcohol, drugs, and casual sex are readily available and widely accepted as normal. They also know the same thing I knew when we dropped Hillary off at college all those years ago: we can't predict how our adult children will respond to temptation, or even what these temptations will look like in their lives.

We cannot predict these things. But we can pray.

Poised for Prayer

I like what R. A. Torrey said about prayer in his time-tested book *How to Pray*. "Prayer," he says, "is God's appointed way for obtaining things, and the great secret of all lack in our experience, in our life and in our work is neglect of prayer."[4] Torrey's book is considered a classic, but he's not the one who came up with the link between asking and receiving. That was God's idea, and over and over again in the Bible, we see God commanding his people to pray—at all times, in all situations, and without giving up.[5]

I think one of the keys to praying effectively at all times

---

4. R. A. Torrey, *How to Pray* (Chicago: Revell, 1900), 9.
5. See, for example, Luke 18:1; 1 Thessalonians 5:17; Ephesians 6:18.

and in all situations is to be *destination* oriented, rather than *process* oriented—and to leave room for God to move however he chooses. The goal when we pray our kids through the transitions of their twenties and on into their grown-up lives is that they will have a saving relationship with Jesus, one that increasingly informs and animates their thoughts, words, and deeds.

Some of our children will get to God (or get *back* to God) by walking the straight and narrow; for others, the path may be crooked, painful, and even sometimes dangerous. I talked to one mom who is convinced that God sometimes takes our kids down paths we would not have chosen to keep us from patting ourselves on the back. "We cannot glory-steal from God," she says. "When our kids come to Christ in a way that only he could have arranged because it looks *nothing* like we would have hoped for or envisioned, we are much more inclined to give him the credit."

Prayer Principle

We cannot glory-steal from God.

When you pray for your adult children in this big-picture way—trusting him to lead them to salvation, no matter how many detours they take or how many times they may get tripped up along the way—remember that they aren't the only ones who will face temptation. We will too.

We'll be tempted to blame ourselves for our kids' mistakes and to second-guess our parenting choices.

We'll be tempted to live in the world of regrets and "if onlys"—as though God cannot redeem our kids' failures (or ours).

And when it looks like nothing is happening and we start to get tired, we'll be tempted to give up on the power of prayer.

But let's not.

When Jesus went to the cross, God showed us his love. When he rose from the dead, God showed us his power. Neither of these things has changed over the years. We may grow weary, but God never does—and he promises that, at the proper time, we will reap a harvest if we do not give up. He says that our labor in the Lord (which includes our prayers) is never in vain.[6] It doesn't matter whether the bad choices belong to our kids or to us, or how big our sin is. God loves us. And his grace has us covered.

Remember what I told my dad back when I jumped headlong into the college party culture? I still like the idea that "grace abounds even more," but I looked up Romans 5:20 in *The Message*, and as I pray my children (and myself) through life's temptations and stumbles, I think I like this translation even better: "When it's sin versus grace, grace wins hands down."

---

6. See Isaiah 40:28; Galatians 6:9; 1 Corinthians 15:58.

Prayers You Can Use

For Yourself

Heavenly Father . . .

You are the God of hope. Fill my heart with all joy and peace as I trust in you, so that I may overflow with hope by the power of the Holy Spirit.   Romans 15:13

Help me to see the trials that _____ goes through as part of your big-picture plan to make him mature and complete, not lacking anything.   James 1:2–4

Equip me to stand firm in prayer for my child, knowing that this labor is not in vain.   1 Corinthians 15:58

For Your Children

Heavenly Father . . .

Show _____ that the party culture is one that seeks to steal and kill and destroy, but that you came so that she could enjoy life and have it in abundance—to the full, overflowing.   John 10:10 AMP

Cause _____ to get rid of all the filth and evil in his life and humbly accept the word you planted in his heart, which has the power to save him.   JAMES 1:21 NLT

Make _____'s steps firm, and cause her to delight in you. When she stumbles, do not let her fall; uphold her with your hand.   PSALM 37:23–24

When _____ faces consequences for his actions, may he realize that no discipline seems pleasant at the time, but painful—but that it will produce a harvest of righteousness and peace in his life.   HEBREWS 12:11

Be faithful to _____. Do not allow the temptations of the party culture to be more than she can stand, but show her the way out.   1 CORINTHIANS 10:13

May _____ know and accept this truth: wine is a mocker and beer a brawler; whoever is led astray by them is not wise.   PROVERBS 20:1

Make _____ alert and sober-minded. Her enemy the devil prowls around like a roaring lion looking for someone to devour. Help her resist him and stand firm in the faith.   1 PETER 5:8–9

Instead of craving drugs, sex, or alcohol, may _____ hunger and thirst for righteousness, actively seeking right standing with you, so that he will be completely satisfied.
                                          MATTHEW 5:6 AMP

May _____ live a decent life, not participating in the darkness of wild parties and drunkenness or any immoral living, but clothing herself with the presence of the Lord Jesus Christ.   ROMANS 13:13–14 NLT

As _____ matures in his adult life, help him flee the evil desires of youth and pursue righteousness, faith, love, and peace, along with those who call on the Lord out of a pure heart.   2 TIMOTHY 2:22

Teach _____ to number her days and recognize how few they are. Help her to spend them as she should.
                                          PSALM 90:12 TLB

Prompt _____ to call on you, and answer him. Be with him in trouble, deliver him, and honor him. Satisfy him with long life, and show him your salvation.
                                          PSALM 91:15–16

CHAPTER 18

Praying for Protection from Sexual Sin

Do not conform to the pattern of this world, but be transformed by the renewing of your mind.

ROMANS 12:2

When I told one of my daughters that I was writing a chapter about sexual sin, she looked doubtful. "Aren't you writing this book for parents of *adult* children?" she asked. "And didn't you cover that stuff in the book you wrote about teens?"

The answer to her first question is yes. I *am* writing for parents of adults. But the implication behind the question—that at some point, parents quit praying about things like sexual sin or promiscuity in their children's lives—made me stop to think: Is there a point at which we throw in the towel on this one, either because our kids are happily married (and therefore seemingly sexually "safe") or because "what's done is done" (and besides, they are old enough to make their own decisions about what they do with their bodies)?

Several parents told me they had, in fact, stopped praying for their children's sexual protection and purity, choosing to focus their prayers on other, more visible or immediate needs: getting a job, finding a marriage partner, dealing with financial pressures and concerns. Others, however, told me they still cry out to God on behalf of their children, asking him to help them stand strong against what feels like a rising cultural tide of promiscuity, pornography, same-sex attraction, adultery, and other threats to their physical, emotional, and spiritual well-being.

Both groups—those who still pray about sexual sin and those who tend to focus on other issues—have this in common: they long for God to give them wisdom and understanding as they relate to their adult children, and they want God to equip them with the ability to love the ones whose choices and lifestyle decisions they don't always like.

So yes, I am writing for parents of adults, regardless of whether or not we see sexual sin as a front-burner prayer issue. All of our kids will make decisions we don't understand or affirm, and at the end of the day, we will all need God's grace to know how to respond and how to love them well.

As for the second question, the one about whether I covered this topic in *Praying the Scriptures for Your Teens*, the answer is . . . sort of. Parents can find encouraging stories and a collection of prayers for protection and purity in that book, but in the dozen or so years since it was written, much has changed. Back then, parents prayed for their daughters' sexual safety; now, several folks told me how concerned they are about the way young women seem to prey on their sons. Back then, college parties were called "mixers"; today, they are often known as "swaps." Back then, pornography was found in magazines and on cable TV; now, thanks to easy access via personal computers and smartphones, it is—in the words of one data analyst—"everywhere."

And perhaps most frighteningly, the cultural stigmas that once provided at least a token defense against sexual sin have all but disappeared. The idea that our adult children will be sexually active before they are married is almost a given; one mom told me that when she dropped her son off at his college dorm, there was only one sign posted in the hallway. It was a university-approved flyer about where students could pick up free condoms during orientation week. "Clearly," this mama observed wryly, "school supplies aren't what they used to be."

We know the pressures and temptations are out there, but as parents who long to see God's best displayed in our adult children's lives, it can be hard to know when to speak up, when to keep silent, and, most importantly, how to pray.

Mitchell is a father who readily admits he had "more questions than answers" when his twenty-eight-year-old daughter told him she was in love with another woman. Having lived and worked in big cities like San Francisco and Los Angeles, Mitchell did not find the homosexual lifestyle surprising or unusual, but he was stunned when he saw Marla's Facebook posts and realized that her frequent companion, Elana, was quite likely more than a "friend."

"Does anybody else notice that Elana is a lesbian?" he asked his wife and son. They agreed she was, but since Marla hadn't yet mentioned anything to the family, Mitchell decided to wait until she raised the subject before he said anything. When she did—more than a year after he had first suspected his daughter was gay—it was a dramatic, tearful confession. Marla knew her parents saw homosexuality as a sin, and she hated the thought that her decision would come between them.

Mitchell felt the same way, and he hastened to reassure his daughter. "You know that Mom and I don't love your lifestyle," he said, "but no matter what you do or don't do, nothing will change the fact that we're family, and we love you."

Privately, though, Mitchell and his wife wrestled with doubt. Had they failed their daughter? Had they done something to cause her to end her relationship with her college boyfriend (a fellow they thought she would marry) and start dating a woman? They knew the church had not always been kind to Marla (she had felt condemnation for some of the choices she'd made as a teenager); had their loyalty to God driven their daughter away?

Mitchell recognized these thoughts as lies and resolved not to entertain them. "We parents take far too much credit when our kids do something great," he said, "and far too much blame when they do something we think is wrong. Neither scenario is accurate; as parents, we just don't have that much influence or control.

"And," he continued, "the reality is that God knew all of this was coming. We all make mistakes, and whether or not we did in this case, we must remember that God is bigger than anything we did or didn't do. I knew the most important thing was not to give the enemy any excuse to drive a wedge into our family, so our top priority was to demonstrate unconditional love for Marla in the same way God does for us."

===== *Prayer Principle* =====

God loves us unconditionally. Ask him to
help you show that same kind of love to your
children, even if you don't like what they do.

Loving their daughter was easy at first, but Mitchell found his resolve tested the next Christmas, when Elana came home with Marla and asked if she could speak with him privately. Mitchell thought he knew what was coming, and sure enough, Elana asked for his blessing to marry Marla.

"I didn't know what to do," Mitchell said. "I couldn't endorse that union, and I found myself at a loss for words. But then the image of Jesus with the woman at the well came to my mind. Jesus knew she had a lot of sin in her life, but his first action toward her was not one of judgment or condemnation; it was one of love."

Taking his cue from that story—which shows Jesus engaging

the woman in a conversation that ultimately led to the salvation of many Samaritans[1]—Mitchell gave Elana his answer: "We love you, and we love Marla," he said. "We believe your relationship with God is the most important thing, and we hope you both will make that a priority in your lives. But whatever you decide and whatever you do, we will always love you."

As Elana and Marla embarked on wedding plans, Mitchell and his wife continued to pray. "We knew it wasn't our job to judge them or try to change them," he said, "so we left that up to God, trusting that what the Bible says is true: God's kindness and patience are intended to lead us to repentance.[2] And since we knew they had both been hurt by condemnation from well-intentioned Christians, we asked God to protect them from that and to put loving people in their lives—people who could point them toward a relationship with Christ."

=== *Prayer Principle* ===

God's kindness leads us to repentance.
Ask God to surround your children with people
who will lovingly point them toward him.

Marla and Elana's story is still unfolding, but Mitchell marvels at the way God has already answered his prayers. Through

---

1. See John 4:1–42.
2. Romans 2:4.

chance encounters of all kinds—on airplanes, at work, and even in a church that Marla began to attend—she is hearing God's Word and feeling his love. For now, the wedding plans are on hold ("They keep getting interrupted," Mitchell says), but no matter what happens, Mitchell and his wife are confident they can trust God to take care of their daughter.

Jena is a mom who would appreciate Mitchell's approach to parenting—and loving—adult children who find themselves caught up in sexual sin. Jena's radar was on high alert after she discovered a pornographic magazine in her son's bedroom, and when she found James looking at the stuff on the family computer, she decided to enlist professional help. A computer expert helped her install filters, and James agreed to meet with a counselor. He also remained active in his youth group and seemed to be pursuing the Lord. By the time he headed off to college a year or so later, Jena hoped they had seen the last of any sort of sexual sin or addiction.

A month or so into the school year, James got ticketed for public intoxication, and as the semester progressed, his grades were so poor that Jena began to fear he would get kicked out of school. Equally concerning was his failure to return texts and phone calls. And when his mom and dad visited the campus on a football weekend, James didn't show up until after the game. Even his sister—a senior at the school—had no idea where he had been. "All of his friends were at the game," she said, "but nobody saw James."

Looking back on that day, Jena concedes that James was most likely spending his time online. "What we know now," she says, "is that he was addicted to pornography. It consumed his time and attention and made him withdraw from other people and activities. At the time, though, we had no idea—and honestly, we were too concerned about his grades and his drinking to even consider that something else might be going on."

James's grades didn't improve, and Jena and Ray decided it didn't make sense to let him return to college the next year. He could, they said, join the military, get a job, or figure out some other way to productively use his time.

James had already landed a summer job as a counselor at a Christian camp, and when he arrived, he learned that the same folks who ran the camp also ran a "gap year" program for students who wanted to add a biblically based year of study to their education, either between high school and college or as an academic alternative to college. To James, that sounded better than enlisting or getting a job, and with his parents' blessing, he filled out an application to the program and was accepted.

It was halfway through the summer, and everything seemed to be going well. Alcohol wasn't available at the camp where James worked, so that wasn't a problem. And he seemed to be thriving in his role as a counselor, growing in his own faith as he encouraged the campers to grow in theirs. Jena and Ray didn't know what the future held, but they had to admit that James seemed to be getting his life straightened out.

Then came the counselors' time off. Like the rest of the staff, James opted to leave the campground and check into a nearby hotel for some much-needed rest. When Ray got the family cell phone bill the next month, he knew something was wrong. James's data usage had skyrocketed during his hotel stay. He had, it turned out, spent the weekend downloading pornography.

"It was awful," Jena said. "It was embarrassing and shameful, and we were all crying.

"But it was also a relief, in a way," she said. "I think James was happy his secret had finally been exposed. He knew what he was doing was wrong; he was just too ashamed to admit it or to ask for help. But when the pieces fell into place—when we realized why he hadn't been communicating and why his grades had gotten so bad—it was like we got a fresh start on solving the puzzle."

Jena and Ray feared that when the gap-year program staff heard about James's addiction (and they knew it had to be confessed), they wouldn't let him come. But in a move that beautifully mirrored God's grace, the program director invited James to continue as planned—only with an added emphasis on discipleship and accountability, as well as a willingness to deal with the underlying issues that had made him withdraw from family and friends and turn to pornography and alcohol.

Within just a few months, Jena and Ray sensed a change in their son. He became more communicative, and when he came home for Christmas, his whole demeanor was different. "He wanted to hang out with us and talk about what he was learning,"

Jena said. "It was as if a light had turned on, like the darkness and secret shame were gone and he could be himself again."

<hr>

Prayer Principle

Light scatters darkness. Ask God to turn your children from darkness to light and from the power of Satan to God.[3]

<hr>

The following year, James went back to college. Distancing himself from his old fraternity life, he surrounded himself with friends who liked to do things that didn't involve alcohol. He also got involved in a small group at his church and maintained close ties with the counselor from the gap-year program, adding new layers of accountability to his collegiate experience.

"Does he still struggle?" Jena wonders. "I don't know; I think he probably does. And I certainly understand how a sexual addiction can affect future relationships; we've seen the devastating effects of pornography in some of our friends' marriages. But we serve a God who is all about redemption and restoration. God can change us and give us complete freedom. That's where I find my hope."

Of all the prayer verses that Jena has prayed over her son, Romans 12:1–2 is the passage that has become her anchor. "I want James to see his body as holy, and I want him to live in a way that pleases God," she says. "I also pray that his mind will

---

3. Acts 26:18.

be renewed. People will tell you that you can't un-see things, but I know that God has the power to change memories and minds and that he can redeem us, physically, mentally, and spiritually."

Poised for Prayer

Listening to Mitchell and Jena tell me their stories, I couldn't help but empathize with their pain. Like so many other moms and dads I talked to, their sadness was compounded by humiliation, confusion, and the sense that somehow they had failed as a parent.

Bestselling author Lysa TerKeurst understands this hurt. As a mom to five children, she has seen her share of "the unexpected" in parenting, the times when doing the "right" things don't produce a child who sticks to the "straight and narrow."

And when that happens, she tells us, "You know what I am tempted to do as a mom? Draw a straight line from my child's wrong choice to my weakness in mothering. That will just about kill a mama. Crack her heart open and fill it with paralyzing regret of the past and fear for the future."[4]

Haven't we all been there? Our child makes a bad decision—she veers off the good-girl path—and we blame ourselves. We let our identity get wrapped up in our kids, and we worry about what other people will think of us. We lose sight of the

---

4. Lysa TerKeurst, *The Best Yes: Making Wise Decisions in the Midst of Endless Demands* (Nashville: Nelson, 2014), 218.

destination—our child's relationship with Christ—and focus on the detours, the things we wish they (or we) didn't have to go through. And we wonder what we could have done differently.

But what if that's not how God sees it? What if, instead of focusing on our weaknesses and fears, he is giving us the opportunity to trust him and to let his strength become our strength in the hard places of parenting? Here's the question Lysa asks:

> What if God said, "What mama is strong enough, persevering enough, tough enough to bend without breaking under the weight of the choices this child will make? What mama is willing to be humbled to the point of humiliation, yet not blinded to the wisdom found like diamonds in dirty places? What mama will not just pray about this child but will truly pray this child all the way through their stuff? What mama will be courageous enough to let Me write her child's story?"[5]

In this book, you have met moms—and quite a few dads—who are letting God write their kids' stories. None of the stories are finished yet. Our kids are going to mess up, and so will we. But that's okay. God is all about redeeming our failures, giving us second chances, and covering our mistakes.

Perhaps nowhere in the entire Bible is this redemption story

---

5. Ibid.

so magnificently portrayed as it is in the book of Hosea. You may know how it goes: God tells the prophet Hosea to marry a promiscuous woman, and even though she continues to be unfaithful, Hosea doesn't give up on her or abandon her. At one point, Hosea even has to buy his wife back, redeeming her out of some sort of slavery. The whole narrative is a beautiful metaphor for the way God feels about us. He knows our hidden flaws and sees our secret sins, and yet he refuses to abandon us. He wants to transform us through the powerful experience of his love.

Unlike most of the temptations our kids will face, sexual sin is one that can often be cultivated in secret. But God sees. He knows. And the example he offers in Hosea—pursuing us, buying our freedom, and emphasizing the person we are meant to be instead of the person we are—provides a template for the way we can love and pray for our adult children. God's plan is the same thing as our prayer: We want them to "come back chastened to reverence before GOD and his good gifts, ready for the End of the story of his love."[6]

---

6. Hosea 3:5 MSG.

Prayers You Can Use

For Yourself

Heavenly Father . . .

When my child is caught in a sin, may I live by the Spirit and restore him gently. Help me to watch myself too, so that I am not also tempted.   GALATIANS 6:1

Teach me to pray in the Spirit, with all kinds of prayers and requests. May I be alert and always keep praying for my children.   EPHESIANS 6:18

Relieve the troubles of my heart and free me from my anguish about my child. Look on my affliction and my distress, and take away all my sins—my parenting mistakes, my failure to trust you, my desire for control, my _____.   PSALM 25:17–18

For Your Children

Heavenly Father . . .

Let _____ have nothing to do with the fruitless deeds of darkness.   EPHESIANS 5:11

Be faithful to _____. Do not let her be tempted beyond what she can bear. And when she is tempted, provide a way out. 1 CORINTHIANS 10:13

Cause _____ to offer his body as a living sacrifice, holy and pleasing to you. Do not let him conform to the pattern of this world, but may he be transformed by the renewing of his mind. ROMANS 12:1–2

Create in _____ a pure heart, and renew a steadfast spirit within her. Let her sense the nearness of your presence. Restore her joy, and give her a spirit that is willing to obey you. PSALM 51:10–12

Teach _____ to take every one of his thoughts captive and make it obedient to Christ. 2 CORINTHIANS 10:5

Do not let _____ offer any part of herself to sin as an instrument of wickedness or as a slave to any sort of impurity; rather, may she offer herself to God as an instrument of righteousness. ROMANS 6:12–19

Cause _____ to recognize that you are patient and kind, and instead of taking those things for granted, let him be led by them to repentance. ROMANS 2:4

May _____ look to you and be radiant; may her face never be covered with shame.   PSALM 34:5

May _____ have nothing to do with sexual immorality, impurity, lust, and evil desires.   COLOSSIANS 3:5 NLT

Prompt _____ to flee from sexual immorality, so that he will not sin against his own body, which is a temple of the Holy Spirit.   1 CORINTHIANS 6:18–19

Do not let _____'s heart be drawn to evil, so that she takes part in wicked deeds.   PSALM 141:4

Lead _____ by your Spirit, so that he will not gratify the desires of the flesh—sexual immorality, impurity, debauchery, drunkenness, orgies, and the like. May his life be marked by love, joy, peace, forbearance, kindness, goodness, faithfulness, gentleness, and self-control.

GALATIANS 5:16–23

CHAPTER 19

Praying for Recovery from an Addiction

He has sent me to bind up the brokenhearted,
to proclaim freedom for the captives
and release from darkness for the prisoners.

ISAIAH 61:1

Before I wrote *Praying the Scriptures for Your Children*, I surveyed more than a hundred parents about what they wanted God to do for their families. I used their answers to shape the table of contents, and if you've seen the book, you know it covers everything from character traits like wisdom and compassion, to good relationships with siblings and friends, to long-term blessings like discovering a God-given purpose in life.

When I did the follow-up book (*Praying the Scriptures for Your Teens*), the chapters just sort of came tumbling out in a hormonal rush, with prayers that addressed concerns like teenage driving, dating relationships, time online, choices in things like music and attire, and a few really tough issues like depression and self-injury.

Now, with four grown children of my own, as well as a handful of godchildren and other young adults who are regularly on my prayer radar, I thought I knew what my peers would want in a book about praying for their adult children. And in many cases, I did. I wasn't surprised, for instance, when parents told me they were concerned about their kids' jobs, marriages, and finances. I knew that health issues—both physical and mental—weighed heavy on people's minds. And of course, given all the expanding families we saw each year in the Christmas cards, I figured I'd need to include at least one chapter about praying for your grandchildren.

What I wasn't prepared for was the number of people who broached the subject of addiction. It didn't matter if I was at a Bible study or a cocktail party; when people heard I was writing a book about praying for adult children, somebody almost always asked a version of the same question: You are writing about alcoholism, right? You are dealing with drug use, aren't you? You do know that heroin addiction is huge among young adults, don't you?

Honestly, I didn't. I guess I live in a bubble, because I had written about protection from drinking and drugs in the teens' book, and I figured that once our kids navigated the rocky waters of high school and college, most of them would find smoother sailing. And the majority of them probably do. But as I listened to the confidings of praying parents from all over the country, many of whom were trusting God against all odds and in the face of unimaginable grief, I realized the depth and breadth of what feels like—and what actually is—an epidemic of substance abuse and addiction. And I felt like my heart would break.

I heard about the star athlete sidelined by injury who, having lost both her physical strength and her sense of identity, found herself addicted to painkillers.

I saw a family picture with the clean-cut, smiling nephew who, after rising to the top of his recruiting class with a big-city consulting firm, overdosed on heroin.

I talked with the mom of a beautiful thirty-two-year-old woman whose marriage was crumbling under the strain of her alcohol addiction.

And I read an article in our newspaper about how users of heroin and other opioids say that the addiction is so powerful it leaves them unable to resist it, even at the risk of their own death. "It's almost at the level of instinct," one doctor said. And get this: he compared an addict's compulsion to use drugs as being about as strong as a parent's to protect his or her child. "You could tell a parent you can't comfort or protect your child or something bad will happen," he said. "It would drive them crazy."[1]

That line undid me. I know how much I love my kids, and how intense my desire is to protect them. Pit that compulsion against an equally powerful force bent on their destruction, and

---

1. Jane Harper, "Virginia Beach Medics Have Revived the Same 18 Opioid Overdose Victims Twice This Year," *Virginian-Pilot*, December 12, 2016, http://pilot online.com/news/local/crime/virginia-beach-medics-have-revived-the-same-opioid -overdose-victims/article_ff2ac9df-99c7-5d27-bb51-8c735f48f24f.html (accessed April 11, 2017).

it's not hard to imagine the fear and grief that can crush a parent's heart when his or her child suffers from addiction.

JoEllen knows that pain. She's a woman who prayed her son through every conceivable boy-brained scheme and adventure, knowing that some of his antics fell outside the bounds of common sense—but never dreaming that his affinity for pushing the limits would land him in a rehab facility before he was thirty years old.

=========== *Prayer Principle* ===========

Addiction is a formidable enemy, but the weapons we fight with—including prayer—have divine power to demolish strongholds.[2]

"Bryson has always been really fun-loving and social," JoEllen said, "and when he went away to college, we were not surprised to see him get involved in a few clubs and campus organizations where drinking was pretty much a backdrop to whatever else was going on. He had the good sense to surround himself with some pretty high-achieving and squared-away kids, so we weren't too concerned about the partying, at least not at first."

JoEllen's unease grew during Bryson's senior year. Her daughter, Becky, had visited the campus and reported seeing Bryson with a black eye, something he said was the result of a

---

2. 2 Corinthians 10:4.

wrestling match. Becky wasn't so sure. "I think he got so drunk that he couldn't walk and he fell," she told her mom. "At least that's what one of his fraternity brothers said. But when I asked Bryson about it, he said I was crazy."

Alcoholism ran in JoEllen's family, and her fears that Bryson might be drinking too much were confirmed on graduation weekend when his best friend, Cole, pulled her aside. "I didn't want to say anything, but some of the guys and I have wondered if we needed to do some sort of an intervention, and I got nominated to talk to you."

"An intervention?" JoEllen didn't like how that sounded.

"Or something. I know we're all excited for graduation, and everyone is celebrating, but it's like Bryson is in another world. He's getting blackout drunk every night, and he's missed a bunch of classes and meetings this spring. Maybe he just doesn't want to leave college. I don't know. And like I said, I didn't want to have to tell you . . ."

"No," JoEllen said. "It's okay. I'm glad you did." She forced herself to smile, thanked Cole for his friendship, and then went in search of Bryson's stepdad, who was talking with a group of happy parents about their kids' plans for the future.

"Let's just get through this weekend," he said when he heard her concern, "and then we can talk to Bryson at home."

JoEllen had regularly prayed the Scriptures for her children, and she knew a lot of verses by heart. But standing there amid a swirl of caps and gowns, nothing came to mind. "I just don't know what to do, Lord," was all she could think to say. "We need your help."

At home, Bryson made light of his parents' concerns. "Everyone drinks in college," he said. "I'm twenty-three—it's not like it's illegal. I know you're worried about me, but you shouldn't be. I'm moving out; I've got a job; and I'll be fine.

"And besides," he teased, "aren't you supposed to start worrying about me getting a girlfriend now? Isn't that what parents want their sons to do once they get out of college?"

JoEllen had to admit that her son seemed fine. He loved a good party, sure, but with college behind him and a job lined up with a tech company in Seattle, things were sure to settle down. And hopefully his faith, which had burned brightly in high school, would reignite once he entered the grown-up world.

And for the next two years, that's exactly what seemed to be happening. Bryson got a promotion, dated a few girls who sounded (to JoEllen, anyway) like they had potential, and had even gone to church a few times. But when he came home for Thanksgiving, she could tell that something was not right.

Bryson had lost weight. He said he wasn't hungry and complained of stomach cramps. And JoEllen couldn't be sure, but it looked like his skin was reddening a little bit, which she knew to be a telltale sign of excessive drinking. Maybe he was just under a lot of stress at work. She hoped that was it.

JoEllen spent Thanksgiving morning in the kitchen, preparing a feast of family favorites. Her husband puttered in and out, sampling things and offering advice. Bryson hadn't shown up, and JoEllen assumed he was jet-lagged and getting some much-needed rest. But when the time came for them to leave for her parents' house to meet up with their extended family for the big meal, she grew a little annoyed and dispatched Becky to rouse her brother.

Moments later, Becky returned. Bryson was in his room, but he wasn't asleep; he was drunk and in no condition to come to a family meal.

"We left without him," JoEllen told me, "and it was awful. We told everyone that he was sick. And when we got home that night, I was too upset to see him. I know what alcoholism can do to a family—I'd seen it with my dad—and I knew Bryson needed help. But at that point I couldn't take it. I just went to bed."

The next morning, Bryson showed up at the breakfast table, his eyes red from crying. "I am so, so sorry," he said. "I know I have a problem. But I don't know what to do."

Fortunately, JoEllen did. The pastor who had helped her father get into a recovery program had retired, but he still lived in town, and she gave him a call. After talking with Bryson, the pastor recommended a residential treatment facility. JoEllen was surprised when Bryson agreed to go, since it meant he'd have to leave his job, but he did.

"We couldn't help him until he admitted he needed it," JoEllen said, "so even though that Thanksgiving was probably the worst day of my life, I am grateful for it as a turning point.

I think it was the beginning of his road to recovery—and maybe of his road back to God as well."

=== *Prayer Principle* ===

God is always at work in our kids' lives, and he can use the worst things to bring about good.

Bryson successfully completed a thirty-day detoxification and stabilization treatment and then moved into a counseling program that addressed addictive behaviors and underlying concerns such as depression and anxiety. He is now in the final phase of his treatment, an outpatient program that uses a twelve-step rehabilitation plan to help people transition back to their families and into the working world.

For her part, JoEllen began attending Al-Anon, the international support group for families and friends of problem drinkers.[3] For her, the group's "Three C's"—*I didn't cause it; I can't control it; I can't cure it*—have become a lifeline to hope and confidence as she has worked to combat the condemning thought that she could have prevented Bryson's problem if she had only been more alert to the warning signs or paid more attention to her family's history of addiction.

JoEllen knows her son's journey to recovery is far from over.

---

3. For more information about Al-Anon, visit www.al-anon.org.

He will have to navigate college reunions, weddings, and a dozen other events that will put him right back in the party scene he left behind when he went to rehab. But like so many of the moms and dads you've met in this book, JoEllen is counting on the truth of verses like Philippians 1:6—that God has begun a good work in Bryson's life, and that he will be faithful to complete it.

=== *Prayer Principle* ===

We cannot control or cure our children's addictions,
but we can hold unswervingly to the hope we profess,
knowing that he who promised is faithful.[4]

"My son is going to face temptation," she says. "That's just part of life. But God promises he will provide a way out, and I'm asking him to be sure Bryson takes it."[5]

Poised for Prayer

Whether she knows it or not, JoEllen's initial prayer for help—the one where she couldn't remember any good verses to pray—*did* echo one of Scripture's most powerful prayers. It's one we can all use, particularly when we don't know how to help our kids or even how to pray for them.

---

4. Hebrews 10:23.
5. 1 Corinthians 10:13.

When King Jehoshaphat found himself besieged by three enemies at once, he proclaimed a fast and cried out to God, contrasting God's power with his utter helplessness. "Lord," he prayed, "you rule over all the kingdoms of the nations. Power and might are in your hand, and no one can withstand you."

And then he got to the heart of the matter: "We have no power to face this vast army that is attacking us. We do not know what to do, but our eyes are on you."[6]

We do not know what to do, but our eyes are on you.

Could there be any more beautiful, practical, all-purpose prayer? When we are powerless to help our kids, God can. When we don't know what to do, he does.

And here's the thing. Our child's addiction might feel like a "vast army"—one that is every bit as powerful as our desire to protect them—but when God enters the fight, the odds change. No one can withstand the power and might of his hand. Our kids are his kids, and his parental instinct is even stronger than ours is. It is to set them free.

If your child is being attacked by addiction—or if you find yourself losing ground in the face of the forces of worry and fear—be assured that God is on your side. He fought on behalf of Israel's children nearly three thousand years ago; he will fight on behalf of our kids today. Let his words—the words spoken to

---

6. 2 Chronicles 20:6, 12.

King Jehoshaphat on the eve of the battle—bring courage and peace to your soul:

> Do not be afraid or discouraged because of this vast army. For the battle is not yours, but God's . . . Take up your positions; stand firm and see the deliverance the LORD will give you . . . Do not be afraid; do not be discouraged. Go out to face them tomorrow, and the LORD will be with you.[7]

Do not be afraid or discouraged.
Take up your position in prayer.
And know that the Lord is with you, and that the battle belongs to him.

---

7. 2 Chronicles 20:15, 17.

Prayers You Can Use

For Yourself

Heavenly Father...

I don't know what to do, but my eyes are on you.

2 CHRONICLES 20:12

When I feel like I've blown it or that I don't have what it takes to bring recovery and healing to my child, let me remember that your grace is sufficient and your strength is made perfect in my weakness.   2 CORINTHIANS 12:9

When my children wander into affliction and addiction, remind me of this reason for hope: Because of your great love we are not consumed, for your compassions never fail. They are new every morning; great is your faithfulness.

LAMENTATIONS 3:19–23

For Your Children

Heavenly Father . . .

Open _____'s eyes; free him from the captivity of addiction; release him from the dungeon of darkness.

ISAIAH 42:6–7

Do not let _____ be tempted beyond what she can bear. When she is tempted by alcohol, drugs, food, or any other addiction, provide a way out, so that she can endure it.

1 CORINTHIANS 10:13

Teach _____ to say no to ungodliness and worldly passions and to live a self-controlled, upright, and godly life.

TITUS 2:12

Remind _____ that you have been tempted in every way and that you empathize with his weakness. Cause him to draw near to you and approach your throne of grace with confidence, so that he will find mercy and grace to help in his time of need.

HEBREWS 4:15–16

May _____ know it is for freedom that Christ has set her free. Equip her to stand firm, not letting herself be burdened by any yoke of slavery.

GALATIANS 5:1

Prompt _____ to give himself to you, so that no other god (drugs, alcohol, sex, gambling, money, etc.) will be his master. Do not let him be enslaved by sin; rather, set him free by your grace. ROMANS 6:14, 17–18

Don't let _____ be drunk with alcohol, which will ruin her life, but fill her instead with your Holy Spirit.

EPHESIANS 5:18 NLT

May _____ be alert and of sober mind, so that he can resist the enemy. Restore _____ and make him strong, firm, and steadfast. 1 PETER 5:8–10

Give _____ wisdom, and set her heart on the right path, so that she will not join those who drink too much alcohol or gorge themselves on food. PROVERBS 23:19–20

Equip _____ to rely on your power to demolish strongholds and take every tempting thought captive and make it obedient to Christ. 2 CORINTHIANS 10:4–5

Set _____ free, so that she will be free indeed.

JOHN 8:36

May _____, being rooted in love, have strength to comprehend the love of Christ that surpasses knowledge and be filled with all your fullness. EPHESIANS 3:17–19

CHAPTER 20

Praying for Your Prodigal

I will give them a heart to know me, that
I am the Lord. They will be my people,
and I will be their God, for they will
return to me with all their heart.

JEREMIAH 24:7

Lauren stared at the photo on her phone, barely comprehending what she saw. It was a picture of her son, William, lying in a hospital bed, his head wrapped in a bloody bandage. He had been assaulted in what he said was a random robbery, and Lauren wanted to believe him. Given what they knew about their son's current lifestyle, she didn't know what to think.

Lauren and her husband, Mike, had been lukewarm about William's plan to move to Chicago when he graduated from college. They understood why a guy from a small town in Alabama would want to spread his wings, but his idea—to launch a neighborhood-based classified-ad service to sell things like used furniture, cars, and household goods—sounded iffy. William had majored in business, but he knew very little about technology and even less about Chicago's diverse neighborhoods. But after a six-month job search closer to home turned up nothing, she and Mike had gotten William a plane ticket and wished him well. Their son was hardworking, creative, and intelligent, so who knew? Maybe he'd be one of the success stories.

And if not, well, what was the worst that could happen?

Lauren had run through a dozen worst-case scenarios in her mind—maybe the business would flop or William would get sick from the city dirt and noise and pollution—but nothing had prepared her for the sight of her son lying in some unknown hospital, more than six hundred miles away. She wished Mike would get home soon; she needed to talk. An orthopedic surgeon, he was usually at the hospital all day on Thursdays, and she hadn't been able to reach him.

Lauren thought back over the past several months. William had burned through most of his start-up money, and then in an effort to recoup his losses, he had started gambling. His drinking, which Lauren and Mike had hoped would lessen once he got out of college, had gotten worse. Lauren didn't know much about William's friends and business associates, but the words from Proverbs 13:20 kept coming to mind: "Walk with the wise and become wise, for a companion of fools suffers harm." Apparently, William had been walking with some fairly serious fools.

When had that started to happen? Lauren didn't know exactly. William had given his life to the Lord at age twelve, and as he grew, so had his faith. He had been a youth group leader in high school, and when the time came to go to college, he elected to live with a Christian roommate. Lauren and Mike were thrilled when William joined a campus Bible study; surely, the friends and the teaching he'd be exposed to there would help guard him against some of the secular philosophies he would encounter in the classroom.

But things hadn't turned out that way. Parties, football games, and study sessions with his classmates filled William's calendar, and he began to drift away from Bible study and other fellowship opportunities. It wasn't as if some atheist had talked him out of his faith; rather, the shift had come gradually as William spent more time with unbelievers than with his Christian friends. And then, almost as if he was looking for an intellectual reason to account for his behavior, William began to question some of the most basic tenets of his faith. Salvation by grace seemed far too simplistic. And the resurrection? Nothing he learned in any of his science classes made that even a remote possibility; it seemed (as William told his parents during his junior year) to be a story designed to bring comfort and hope to people who would grasp at anything to keep their faith alive. Which was fine for them—just not for him.

Mike and Lauren hadn't wanted to alienate their son by revealing the depth of their concern or by arguing against some of his claims. Instead, they welcomed William's questions, pointing him toward authors like Josh McDowell, Lee Strobel, and C. S.

Lewis, apologists whose work they thought might appeal to him on an intellectual level.

"But honestly," Mike had said, after one of their conversations, "I don't think he is looking for evidence to support Christianity. I think it's a moral issue, masquerading as an intellectual one. I think he wants to find a worldview to support his quest for independence and self-sufficiency as he runs away from God, something that will justify his rebellion."

=== *Prayer Principle* ===

Ask God to work in your prodigal's mind and spirit, demolishing arguments and every pretension that sets itself up against the knowledge of God.[1]

The kitchen door opened, snapping Lauren's mind back to the present. It was Mike, home from the hospital where he had been making rounds. Lauren showed him the photo and filled him in on what little she knew.

"He says it's nothing serious," she said. "Some guys jumped him when he was walking home from work. He says they took his wallet . . ."

"Maybe they did," Mike said, "but we aren't sending him any more money."

---

1. 2 Corinthians 10:5.

He picked up the phone and enlarged the photo. "It looks like a good bandage job at least. He'll be okay."

Lauren knew Mike wasn't being callous or insensitive, and that he was hurting just as much as she was. He was just being practical. But for a mom, it wasn't that easy.

"Mike, I want William to come home," she said softly.

"I think he should," Mike agreed, "but we can't make him do anything. He's literally living the life of the prodigal son—he got us to give him some money, and then he went away to a distant city and squandered it all in wild living. For all we know, he has been eating with pigs!"

Lauren knew the story Mike was talking about. It was a parable in Luke 15, one Jesus used to illustrate the heavenly Father's love and the power of redemption. In that story, the son finally comes home, confessing his sins and giving up any claim he had on the family name. "I am no longer worthy to be called your son," he says. "Make me like one of your hired men."[2]

Lauren loved that parable—especially the part where the father sees the son in the distance and, throwing dignity to the wind, runs out to embrace his boy in a very public, very emotional reunion. It was perhaps the best illustration she knew of to show how God feels about us, and how utterly ecstatic he is when we acknowledge our own unworthiness and turn to him.

Missing from the story, though, was an account of the

---

2. Luke 15:19.

prodigal's mother. Surely, she had longed to hear from her boy, to receive some word that he was at least alive. And certainly, when she heard the sound of his greeting, her heart would have leaped right along with her husband's. Who knows? She might have even beaten him down the street.

Lauren knew the story wasn't about a literal, historical family, one with a real mom and dad. But if it had been, Lauren knew one thing for sure: that mama would have been praying.

=========== *Prayer Principle* ===========

God knows what it's like to grieve over a prodigal child—and to rejoice over his return.

Listening to Lauren and Mike, I was reminded of any number of similar accounts people shared with me as I worked on this book. Mothers and fathers told me about their kids' faith; how they'd grown up in the church, attended Christian camps, or gone on mission trips; and read The Chronicles of Narnia at bedtime. These parents, like so many I interviewed, had done everything in their power to produce Christian kids—and sometimes, as one parent put it, "A plus B really did equal C." But sometimes (a lot of times, actually), it didn't.

"My daughter looks at the quality of our lives," one father confided, "and she says that's what she wants in her life: deep, Christ-centered friendships where people live in community and support one another. But unless God reveals himself personally to her, she says she isn't interested in him. She doesn't want to live by faith; she says she has to see it."

"My son feels like Christianity was forced on him when he was a child," another mother said. "He resents the fact that we sent him to a Christian school and asked him to memorize Scripture, because he sees that as too legalistic. But we take comfort in knowing that God's Word is in his heart, and that the Holy Spirit can use it to counsel him. And since John 6:44 says that no one comes to Christ unless the Father draws him, we are asking God to draw our son to Christ."

"I have three prodigal children," said yet another mother, "and I pray for all of them. I can't control what they think or how they act; all I can do is love them and trust God. So that's what I'm trying to do."

I think my favorite comment came from a mom whose daughter has walked a path no parent would choose for a child. Looking at all of the bad decisions (and tragic consequences) the girl has experienced, and stacking those things up against verses like Genesis 50:20 ("You intended to harm me, but God intended it for good"), this sweet mama summed up her perspective like this: "I don't know what God is doing in my daughter's life, or why she does the things she does. All I can figure is that she is working on her testimony. And it's shaping up to be a good one."

For parents who've staked their trust in the Lord (and for those who believe, as author Max Lucado puts it, that "we see a perfect mess; God sees a perfect chance to train, test, and teach"[3]), the idea that our kids are still "working on their testimonies" is a lifeline to hope. And it's not just *their* stories that are still being written; Lauren and Mike don't know what the future holds for William, but they'd be the first to tell you that his experience has shaped their own spiritual journey in a powerful way.

"We've prayed more than ever before," Lauren told me, "and we've learned to wait on God. It's hard not to let fear and worry cloud the picture, but the more we look into the bright light of God's love, the more those dark things are obliterated. This trouble has been a gateway for us to get to know God better; our prayer is that it will also be a gateway for William."

Prayer Principle

The light of God's love is what scatters the darkness.
Tether your prayers to the brightness of his promises.

"We've learned that we are completely helpless," Mike added. "We cannot change or control our kids' lives; all we can do is trust in a God who has given us great and precious promises."

Mike is right. We are helpless, at least insofar as it comes to dictating the way our adult children think and behave. Many of them are out of our reach, physically, emotionally, and spiritually.

3. Max Lucado, *You'll Get through This: Hope and Help for Your Turbulent Times* (Nashville: Nelson, 2013), 10.

But they are not out of God's—and he invites us to join him in the work he is doing, through prayer. We are not helpless there; even when we have no idea how to pray, God has us covered. "The Spirit helps us in our weakness," Paul writes in Romans 8:26. "We do not know what we ought to pray for, but the Spirit himself intercedes for us through wordless groans."

Poised for Prayer

As we partner with God and pray for our prodigals, let's keep a few key points in mind:

First, *God knows our pain*. He knows exactly what it's like to love a child, to teach him to walk, to feed him, and to kiss his cheek—and then to have that child grow up and walk away, choosing a world marked by bondage, destruction, and violence.[4] All of the grief, anger, and frustration that we experience as parents are bound up in his heart as well. And, despite how the story of the prodigal son plays out in Luke (with no "mom" in the picture), it's not just the love of a *father* that God understands. Consider this lament, and how it reflects the way *mothers* are wired: "Jerusalem, Jerusalem, you who kill the prophets and stone those sent to you, how often I have longed to gather your children together, as a hen gathers her chicks under her wings, and you were not willing."[5]

---

4. See Hosea 11:1–11.
5. Matthew 23:37.

God knows what it's like to ache for a child. He knows our pain.

Next, *God loves our kids, even more than we do.* Lauren told me that, as she cried out to God on William's behalf, it was hard to get past the fact that it was *her* son who had done all of this awful stuff. As she sat there, wondering what she had done wrong or how her boy could have gone so far afield, God interrupted her thoughts. *William is my son too*, she sensed him say, *and my love for him is not diminished one bit by anything he has done or will ever do.*

God loves our kids, no matter what.

Third, *God really has given us "great and precious promises"*—promises specifically designed to enable us to live godly lives.[6] When we pray these promises—praying God's Word over our children—we can do it with confidence, knowing that he is patient, "not wanting anyone to perish, but everyone to come to repentance."[7] And if you worry that your kids missed out because maybe you were not a praying parent when they were young or because you never took them to church or whatever, consider what Jesus said: "I have not come to call the righteous, but sinners to repentance."[8] Your child is a sinner? Hooray. He or she is the one God came to call. That's the whole point.

God's promises are true. Let's use them with confidence.

---

6. 2 Peter 1:3–4.
7. 2 Peter 3:9.
8. Luke 5:32.

And finally, as we consider how to behave toward our children, particularly as we try to navigate the thin space between discipline and grace and as we wrestle with our own feelings of anger and hurt, *let's take our cue from our heavenly Father*. It's not just our kids who have wandered: "We all, like sheep, have gone astray."[9] We've all walked in the prodigal's shoes ("I am the prodigal son every time I search for unconditional love where it cannot be found," writes Henri Nouwen[10]), and we all need God's mercy and grace. And God, in turn, has shown us exactly how to live. We must, he says, be "joyful in hope, patient in affliction, faithful in prayer."[11]

Let's ask God to help us do that—to be joyful, patient, and faithful in prayer. Let's ask him to help us see our kids through his eyes and love them the way he does. And let's, in faith, look forward to the day we'll join our voices with our heavenly Father's, saying, "We had to celebrate and be glad, because this brother of yours was dead and is alive again; he was lost and is found."[12]

---

9. Isaiah 53:6.

10. Henri J. M. Nouwen, *The Return of the Prodigal Son: A Story of Homecoming* (New York: Continuum, 1995), 39.

11. Romans 12:12.

12. Luke 15:32.

Prayers You Can Use

For Yourself

Heavenly Father . . .

Help me be kind and patient with my children, gently instructing them when they oppose your truth. Change their hearts. 2 TIMOTHY 2:24–25 NLT

Equip me to be joyful in hope, patient in affliction, and faithful in prayer. ROMANS 12:12

Don't let me be anxious, but help me to be thankful as I share my requests with you. May your peace guard my heart and my mind. PHILIPPIANS 4:6–7

For Your Children

Heavenly Father . . .

No one can come to Christ unless the Father draws him. Draw _____, Lord. JOHN 6:44

Summon _____ by name. Strengthen him, even though he does not acknowledge you, so that he will know you alone are the Lord.   ISAIAH 45:4–6

Grant _____ repentance, and lead her to know the truth. May she come to her senses and escape from the trap of the devil, who has taken her captive to do his will.

2 TIMOTHY 2:25–26

Rescue _____ and protect him. Cause him to acknowledge your name. Be with _____ in trouble; deliver him and honor him.   PSALM 91:14–15

Work in _____'s mind and spirit, demolishing arguments and every pretension that sets itself up against the knowledge of God.   2 CORINTHIANS 10:5

Open _____'s eyes. Turn her from darkness to light, and from the power of Satan to God, so that she may receive forgiveness of sins and a place among those who are sanctified by faith.   ACTS 26:18

Bring _____ home. Cleanse him from all his impurities. Remove his heart of stone, and give him a heart of flesh. Put your Spirit in _____; move him to follow you and keep your laws.   EZEKIEL 36:24–27

May _____ experience godly sorrow that brings repentance, the kind that leads to salvation and leaves no regret.   2 CORINTHIANS 7:10

Create in _____ a pure heart. Renew a steadfast spirit in her. Do not cast _____ from your presence or take away your Holy Spirit; instead, restore the joy of her salvation and make her willing to obey you.

PSALM 51:10–12

Open _____'s heart, so that he will respond to the message of the gospel.   ACTS 16:14

Have compassion on _____, and do not be angry with her. Cause her to hear your voice and return to you, following you as you bring her home.   HOSEA 11:9–11 NLT

When _____ confesses his rebellion and you forgive him, may he rejoice in the knowledge that all his guilt is gone.   PSALM 32:5 NLT

Is Jesus Enough?

*I have no greater joy than to hear that
my children are walking in the truth.*

3 John 4

Is Jesus enough?

That's the question a dear friend asked me one day as we talked about some of the briar patches and thorny places our grown-up kids were facing. Like, if our children struggled with drugs or alcohol or pornography, if they didn't get the job they wanted and went through a lean financial season, or if they married someone we didn't really like or approve of . . . but if, at the end of the day, they found their way to Jesus, would that be okay? Would I be satisfied with that?

I had to think about that one. I didn't *want* to say yes, but I realized my friend was on to something. It *had* to be okay. Because, at the end of the day, none of that other stuff really matters. Good health, fulfilling jobs, and even happy marriages are all temporal, but a saving relationship with Jesus lasts forever. As the psalmist put it, "Whom have I in heaven but you? And earth has nothing I desire besides you. My flesh and my heart may fail, but God is the strength of my heart and my portion forever."[1]

I knew my friend was right (and that the psalmist was too), but you would not have known it by looking at me. A person whose kids are "walking in the truth" (as mine are, thanks be to God) should have joy, right? Someone who knows, deep down, that Jesus really *is* all we need ought not to have her emotions dictated by circumstances, right? *Right?*

But I didn't. I was a blue petunia. I had been praying about several big things for my kids—things having to do with their jobs and living arrangements and relationships—and life wasn't exactly shaping up as I thought it should. In some cases, God seemed to be taking forever; in other cases, he clearly said no.

I felt bad. I felt bad for my kids, and I felt bad for myself. As someone who writes and speaks about God's amazing love and his sovereign power and all the ways he knows what we need, I figured I should be able to handle things like disappointment and rejection without crumbling. But I was blowing it.

And I told God so.

"I feel like a failure," I said. "I know you are powerful and that you love my kids and have a wonderful plan for their lives. I know you have everything under control. I should be happy, not sad or confused. *What's wrong with me?*"

There are lots of ways to hear from God, but the main way I hear him is through Scripture, and he showed me two blessings that day.

---

1. Psalm 73:25–26.

=========== *Prayer Principle* ===========

God doesn't want us to trust in an outcome;
he wants us to trust in him.

The first blessing was that it was okay for me to grieve.
Matthew 5:4 reads, "Blessed are those who mourn, for they
will be comforted." As I sat there, pouring my heart out to God,
I sensed him say, *It's okay. Your sadness and disappointment are
real. Bring them to me, and let me comfort you.*

Pain and rejection and loss—and prayers that don't get
answered like we want them to—feel like such negative things.
But they're not, at least not in God's hands. When our suffering
invites us to press into God—to climb into his embrace the way
our own children did when they were little and needed us to love
them and tend to their hurts—it becomes an agent of beauty.

The second thing God showed me was a little more direct.
Psalm 84:12 reads, "Blessed is the one who trusts in you." I read
that verse and felt like God said, *Jodie, your trust is in the wrong
place. You are trusting in* outcomes—*in the things you think ought
to happen. I want you to trust in* me.

Ahhh. He was right. I had the wrong anchor; no wonder I
found myself drifting.

Jennifer Kennedy Dean writes that God works through the
process of prayer to "expand our vision, to deepen our hunger,
to stretch our faith, and to lift our desires higher. We start

the process desiring something from Him; we end it desiring only Him."[2]

I saw that deepening process played out over and over again in this book. None of the parents I interviewed would wish their stories on anyone, but almost all of them said the same thing: Their challenges had forced them to take their eyes off of outcomes, because the outcomes were not there. But the yearning—the hunger for something that would satisfy—still was. And the more they pressed in, the more they realized that the yearning was not for an outcome after all; the yearning was simply for Jesus.

When this happens—when our confidence becomes rooted in God himself instead of in some particular outcome—we gain freedom from things like anxiety, insecurity, and fear. We gain joy. We gain peace.

So that's what I'm asking God to help me do—to help me put my confidence, my trust, and my delight in him rather than in any blessing or gift he might provide. And I'm asking him to do that for my children and their spouses too.

Several of the adult children you've read about, including my own, are learning what it means to wait on God, to trust him when the answer seems long in coming (or when it comes and it's not the answer they wanted). For them, perhaps even more than for us, this is hard. They represent a generation accustomed to instant gratification, whether it comes from a text message,

---

2. Jennifer Kennedy Dean, *Live a Praying Life* (Birmingham, AL: New Hope, 2010), 76.

a Facebook post, or an Amazon next-day delivery. In order to wait well—to walk without fainting and run and not grow weary in the dark or dry places of life—they are going to need help. They are going to need God's Spirit to go to work in their lives.

In my previous books, I included chapters that focused on praying for your child's character—for things like perseverance, kindness, and self-control. I didn't repeat those topics here because, honestly, the need for these God-given attributes is implicit. You can't get through a job hunt without perseverance; you can't navigate a marriage without kindness; you can't survive in our party culture without a hefty dose of self-control.

In the preceding chapters, you've read dozens of character-shaping prayers for these traits (and plenty of others, including wisdom, compassion, a strong work ethic, an others-centered outlook, and joy). All of these things represent the fruit and the gifts of the Holy Spirit. And as we ask God to bless our kids with these things (even as we ask him to give them good jobs and good health and good friends), let's ask him to shift their focus—and ours—from the gifts to the Giver. Let's pray that our children will fall wholeheartedly in love with Jesus—not because of what he can do, but because of who he is.

Heavenly Father . . .

Whom have we in heaven but you? Work in us and in our children, so that nothing compares to the desire we have for you. Be the strength of our hearts and our portion forever. Amen.   Psalm 73:25–26

Acknowledgments

United States Senate Chaplain Barry Black says he had "about forty-five seconds' worth of prayer material"—until he became a parent. Then, propelled by his sense of need, he began making his voice heard in heaven.

I know what exactly what he means. And I am grateful beyond measure for the prayers of those who have come alongside me in my need, making their voices heard, not just for my children, but also for me as I tried to "bring up" this book.

To my beloved family at Galilee Church (especially the Thursday Bible study girls, whose hunger to know and pray and *live* the Scriptures helped shape a lot of what I wrote on these pages) and Father Andy Buchanan (who fielded all of my "Is this right?" queries with unflagging grace)—thank you. You are modern-day Philemons; you ooze joy, and you refresh the hearts of the saints.

And to my faithful Moms in Prayer partners (women who know the power of praying God's Word, and who have stood in the gap on behalf of my family for twenty years); the Empty Nest Summiteers (your friendship comes like water to a dry land, every year); my WWW girls (whose timely encouragement and intercession pushed this book over the finish line); and the strong and precious army of dear friends and family members who offered prayer, advice, and biblical answers to my thorniest questions—thank you. Your names are etched on my heart; your love (and your patience with my incessant texting) brought these pages to life.

And to the team at Zondervan (some of whom I've known almost as long as I've had children), thank you too. It is a privilege to work with editors—Sandy Vander Zicht, Lori Vanden Bosch, and Dirk Buursma—who hold themselves and their authors to a high standard of excellence, whether it's in knowing how to rightly handle Scripture or where a comma should go. Likewise, to the incredibly creative and tech-savvy marketing professionals at C. Grant and Company (especially Julie Busteed and Tiffany Self) and at Yellow Leaf Marketing (Courtney and Danny Rohrdanz)—you are amazing. Thank you for gently bearing with my social media ignorance (who needs *training* to work Facebook?) and for doing your jobs with an Ephesians 4:2 kind of love.

Here's where things get a bit weepy. I don't do mushy well, so I'll just put it out there:

Mom and John, thank you for teaching me what it looks like to love your grown-up kids well, for steadfastly pointing us toward Christ and for *always* being ready, willing, and able to pray. And Billy and Mary Lou, a girl could not ask for a more loving or gracious set of in-laws. Robbie and I want to grow up to be you.

To my children and their spouses—Hillary and Charlie, Annesley and Geoff, Virginia, and Robbie—I love you. And I love talking to God about you. Thank you for letting me share your stories, for loving me through (and in spite of) the writing process, and for all the ways that you keep on improving my prayer life. Dad's too. We adore you.

Speaking of "Dad"—Robbie, as a husband and father you are the living, breathing embodiment of Ephesians 3:20. I began praying for you when I was thirteen years old, and when he brought you into my life, God did more—immeasurably more!—than all I could ever ask or imagine. He is so beyond good. And you take my breath away.

And finally . . .

To the courageous, honest, and incredibly faithful mothers and fathers who told me their stories—knowing that I could change your names but not your emotions—you make me cry happy tears. Thank you for sharing your hearts. Thank you for your faithfulness in parenting. Thank you for your prayers.

You are God's beloved . . . and so are your children.